VIKRAM SETH'S

FROM
HEAVEN
LAKE

"Kathmandu is vivid, mercenary, religious, with small shrines to flower-adorned deities along the narrowest and busiest streets; with fruitsellers, flutesellers, hawkers of postcards and pornography; shops selling Western cosmetics, film rolls and chocolate; or copper utensils and Nepalese antiques. Film songs blare out from the radios, car horns sound, bicycle bells ring, stray cows low questioningly at motorcycles, vendors shout out their wares. I indulge myself mindlessly: buy a bar of Tobler marzipan, a corn-on-the-cob roasted in a charcoal brazier on the pavement (rubbed with salt, chili powder and lemon); a couple of love story comics, and even a *Reader's Digest*. All this I wash down with Coca Cola and a nauseating orange drink, and feel much better for it."

VINTAGE DEPARTURES

Vikram Seth

FROM HEAVEN LAKE

Travels through Sinkiang and Tibet

VINTAGE BOOKS

A Division of Random House New York

First Vintage Departures Edition,
November 1987

Library of Congress Cataloging-in-Publication Data
Seth, Vikram, 1952–
From Heaven Lake.
(Vintage departures)
Reprint. Originally published:
London: Chatto & Windus, 1983.
1. Sinkiang Uighur Autonomous Region
(China)—Description and travel.
2. Tibet (China)—Description and travel.
3. Seth, Vikram, 1952–   —Journeys—
China—Sinkiang Uighur Autonomous Region.
4. Seth, Vikram, 1952–   —Journeys
—China—Tibet. I. Title.
DS793.S62S38 1987   915.1'50458   87-40067
ISBN 0-394-75218-X (pbk.)

The author gratefully acknowledges Penguin Books Ltd
for permission to quote from *Tao Te Ching*
by Lao Tzu and *The Analects* by Confucius,
both translated and edited by D. C. Lau.

Author photo copyright © 1986 by Mr. Kitty Hazuria

Manufactured in the United States of America
15 14

To the people I met along the way

I am very grateful to Stanford University and the Ford Foundation, who supported me in China for two years.

I would also like to thank Nanjing University, where I was a student for those two years.

Most of all I am indebted to Gabrielle Harris, who among other things typed almost the whole of the manuscript. She was at the same time editor and critic, disciplinarian and friend. Only she can know how valuable were her suggestions, occasional prodding and continuous encouragement.

V.S.

Contents

Contents

Introduction

I am Indian, and lived in China as a student at Nanjing University from 1980–82. In the summer of 1981 I returned home to Delhi via Tibet and Nepal.

The land route – for this was a hitch-hiking journey – from the oases of northwest China to the Himalayas crosses four Chinese provinces: Xinjiang (Sinkiang) and Gansu in the northwestern desert; then the basin and plateau of Qinghai; and finally Tibet. This book is based on the journal I kept while I was on the road.

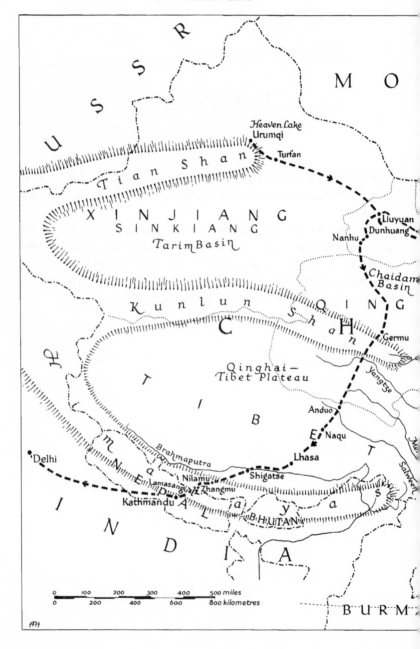

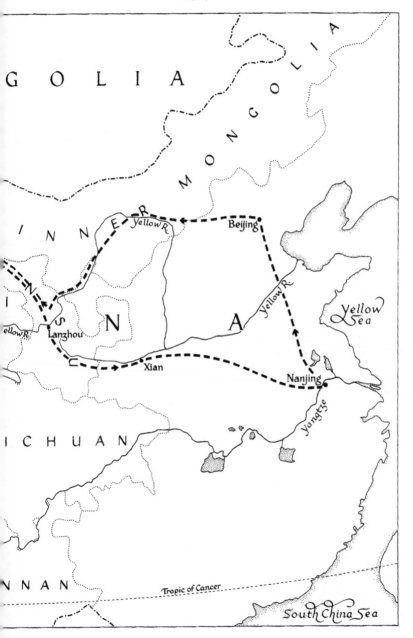

I

Turfan:

July in the desert

The flies have entered the bus, and their buzzing adds to the overwhelming sense of heat. We drive through the town first: a few two-storey buildings of depressing concrete, housing government offices or large shops – foodstores, clothing, hardware. Small street stalls, too, with their wares displayed on the pavement and vendors selling refreshments – glasses of bilious yellow and red liquids, looking increasingly attractive as our thirst builds. Donkey-carts pulled by tired-looking donkeys, pestered by flies and enervated by the dry, breezeless heat, some ridden by young boys with white skull-caps, others standing beside piles of watermelons. Even when they flick their tails, they do so listlessly. It is not long past dawn, and already the heat has struck. And the light, shining on walls and signs – in Chinese, Latin and Arabic scripts – has a painful brilliance.

Turfan; July. The combination is not a happy one, even for someone accustomed to the oven of Delhi as the summer heat builds up over northern India. The only way to remain even tolerably cool in Turfan is to pour cold water on your head and let your hair dry in the air. This happens in minutes and the process can then be repeated.

Turfan lies in a depression in Xinjiang (Sinkiang), the extreme northwest province of China bordering on the Soviet Union. In summer it bakes and in winter it freezes. It is an oasis town, and its agriculture depends on subterranean water-sources under the inclined plains south of a distant range – just visible to us, purple on the horizon. But since everything evaporates so alarmingly fast at the time that irrigation is most needed, an ingenious system has been constructed for the preservation and transportation of this water. We are to see this later today.

As for Xinjiang itself, it is a curious province. The name means 'New Borderland', but the 'new' is as appropriate a modifier as in the 'New Forest'. The area, populated mainly by people quite different from the Hans (who make up more than nine-tenths of China's population), was first 'pacified' by the Chinese some two thousand years ago. Since then it has been an area of Chinese interest dotted with military outposts and, in different periods, tenuously or closely connected with China: sometimes independent, sometimes semi-independent, and sometimes (as now) an integral province of the country. Strictly speaking, it is not a 'province'. The Chinese call it an 'autonomous region'. This is the name for administrative entities of provincial size which are populated largely by minorities, i.e. non-Hans. (Tibet is another such region.) But effective power is entirely in Beijing's hands.

Xinjiang is a desert province, with the huge Tarim Basin at its heart. When it came to this basin, the ancient Silk Route from China to the Mediterranean bifurcated into the northern and southern Silk Routes. These skirted the periphery of the Tarim, to join again at its western end and continue the long traffic from Changan to Antioch. Along these routes – sometimes desert tracks, sometimes not tracks at all but wastes marked by beacon or tower – lay the green nodes of oasis-towns. Here imperial officials, or whoever happened to hold the region at the time, would examine the visas of merchants and travellers, verify their credentials, provide them with permission to hire or buy fresh mounts (usually camels), and allow them to proceed. Along the southern route lie such towns as Yarkand and Khotan. Along the northern lie Turfan and Urumqi. The routes rejoin at Kashgar, in western Xinjiang.

But Kashgar is out of bounds for foreign travellers. Any area too close to the Soviet 'social imperialists' is, and the green-uniformed People's Liberation Army is everywhere in evidence. The treaties of the two imperial, not to say imperialist, powers have left the boundary in some dispute, and their two socialist successors have fought bloodily over it. Furthermore, each side has a 'minority problem' in the area, for the Uighurs and Kazakhs who live in this historical no-man's-land of Central Asia and whose far-ranging communities, settled or nomadic, are scattered on both sides of a border negotiated or contended over by others, feel little sense of allegiance to the Russians who dominate the USSR or the Hans who dominate China.

They are Muslim in culture and religion; cultures based on the Orthodox Church or on Confucianism are equally alien to them. The script of the Uighur language is Arabic. The dress of the people on the streets outside is colourful, unlike the drab ubiquitous blue of eastern China. Their features are more marked, eyes larger, skin browner: they are in fact racially more akin to the Turks than to the Chinese. But China is a multinational state, and sixty per cent of its area is peopled by the six per cent of its minorities. Beijing is not unalive to the reality of minority disaffection and the need to appease or crush it.

One feature apparently shared by the Uighurs and the Hans is the passion for walls. We have passed out of the town centre and are in the residential outskirts. Small mud houses with walled compounds go past, a grape trellis flung over a courtyard, an occasional tall sunflower raising its head over the wall. Claire cuts a Hami melon. It is not sweet, unlike the watermelons and grapes we have been eating ever since we arrived in Turfan. But it is cool, and we are now in the desert again. The minibus (organised for the Foreign Students Office of Nanjing University by the Foreign Affairs Office of Turfan) pants courageously along the straight metalled road, aimed for another oasis in the distance. This lies close to the old capital city of a local kingdom, whose vast ruins of clay wall and clay edifice continue till today to crumble and survive.

A wall, miles long, circles the ruins. There are towers and domes and palaces and ramparts, and a heat and dryness that are breathtaking. Our guide gives us names and dates and they go straight out of my head – evaporate. I walk away by myself, and climb a flight of collapsing steps to the top of a high wall. From here I watch a donkey-cart with a load of grass – green! green! – trundle through the baked ruins to a market in the small settlement beyond. Every few minutes I take a swig from my waterbottle. I am trying to recall how 'Ozymandias' goes when the bus horn reminds me that the group is about to leave. I scramble down, notice I have left my lens-cap at the top of the wall, scramble up – the honking of the horn has become frantic – rush down again and arrive breathless and heat-dazed at the bus.

3

The ruins we have just visited are described as follows in a pictorial guide to Turfan:

The most famous place is Ko Chang Old City. The City is in the south-east of Turpan and is said to be built in 1.B.C. It is lasted until the 14th. Century. In other words, the City has a long history of about 1500 years.

In the ancient time, Ko Chang City acted as an important political, economical and cultural centre. It was also a city along the Silk Route. The City was ruined during a fierce battle which fighting cause is religion.

Before the Muslim invasion and conversion, the area around Turfan was Buddhist. We are now to be taken to some Buddhist temples and monasteries that lie – also in ruins – on the other side of Turfan. When we arrive I look for lizards in the cracked clay crevices, but can see none. The heat is stifling and there is no vegetation except for the sporadic thorny scrub. The buildings are domed, of uncoloured clay, preserved to some extent though dryness, but damaged, I imagine, by the expansion of freezing moisture during cooler months: the clear skies make for a large daily swing in temperature. This site is a long plateau, islanded between the fork and rejoin of a stream far below. Its edges are precipitous, and the braiding stream so far down feeds a brilliant band of green growth. It must have been an enormous task supplying the monastery and temples with water, and I wonder if this place, like Fatehpur Sikri, died for lack of it. I should ask, I suppose; but it will mean a walk back to the guide; and the heat is so intense that I decide to sit in ignorance in the shadow of a wall and stare at a stone.

I am the last one on the bus. 'You are late as usual,' says the guide, an amiable Uighur official who is keener to get us from one tourist attraction to another an hour away than to allow us twenty minutes at the places themselves. He looks at his watch and sucks in his breath. There is a hurried consultation with the driver, after which we descend from the plateau to find ourselves in the desert again.

The three week tour we are on has been organised by Nanjing University for its foreign students: a mixed bunch, though largely from the richer countries, with Japan and the US predominating. During the one or two years we are at Nanjing we study or research our subjects – ranging from philosophy to Chinese literature, from economics to history – usually on leave of absence from our own universities. Nanjing University provides us with facilities and some supervision, but does not grant degrees. During the holidays we are permitted to travel.

The tenor of this trip, though, is beginning to worry me. It is well-organised – the transport, the board, the accommodation, the guides, everything that would be time-consuming and expensive for individuals to arrange has been thought of. Considering the problems of organisation (train tickets, for example, can be booked no earlier than three days in advance) things have gone smoothly. Yet the comfort of being cushioned from these practicalities has brought with it restrictions of two kinds.

The first is inherent in group travel, indeed in any form of organised group activity – a discipline, a punctuality, imposed upon the participants. Every minute I am late for the bus means fifteen wasted person-minutes for the group as a whole. It will not do, I realise, to stare at a stone when Claire and Carlo and Midoragawa and John and Wolfgang and ten others besides are slowly vaporising in the bus. And yet to be hustled by the Group Will into rushing from sight to sight, savouring nothing, is, I'm sure, irksome to all of us.

The second kind of restriction is peculiar to travel in China. The movement of foreigners is tightly controlled, and it is easier to keep an eye on a group than on its scattered members. A travel pass is needed for every place – outside Nanjing – that we foreign students go to. It has to be filled out and signed by the Public Security Bureau (the police). They will certainly refuse, for instance, to put Kashgar on it; the whole of rural China, except for famous scenic spots or – occasionally – model communes, is out of bounds. If you travel in a group, even what is shown within a town is effectively limited to those places to which the guide is willing to take you. By the engaging ploy of keeping you continuously occupied from dawn to sunset he leaves you no time to explore. Our avuncular guide, Abdurrahman, is particularly adept at this. This is stringent enough, but the situation is aggravated by the ever-present phenomenon of *lianxi* – a word as fundamental to an understanding of China as *guiding* (regulations), or *guanxi* (personal connections in official places). Roughly translatable as 'contact' or 'liaison', *lianxi* is absolutely

5

essential for effective action where discretion, personal fiefdoms and a hierarchical system of command exist. Channels for lateral communication are poor in China. If your work-unit wants something done by another work-unit not in its direct line of command, you have one of two choices. Either apply upwards through your hierarchy to a common boss, and then have the order percolate downwards to the other unit, which is time-consuming; or, alternatively, try, through phone calls, visits, common friends, promises of future favours or some other form of *lianxi*, to get them to do what you want.

Since we foreign students are under the care of the Nanjing University teachers accompanying us, and since the group, during its stay in Turfan, travels under the aegis of the Turfan office of the Foreign Affairs Bureau, there are certain proprieties to be observed. If we want to see something – a museum, for instance – we cannot go to the curators ourselves. We speak to our teachers, who *lianxi* with the Foreign Affairs guide, who, after checking with his superiors, will *lianxi* with some representative of the Ministry of Culture, who will talk to the museum authorities. By that time, of course, we will probably have left for another destination. It is also worth noting that in this delicate concatenation a single reasoned, hostile, lazy or timorous 'no' is sufficient to stymie our efforts to do what we want to do, or to see what we want to see.

I do not think that I will be able to tolerate the limitations of group travel much longer. I have already committed myself at Turfan, but at Urumqi I will simply refuse to be shown the sights. Seeing fewer monuments will not distress me. At the birth of this idea I pour a little baptismal water onto my head and feel the cool comfort as it steams off my hair. I drink the last of the water and, more cheerfully than before, face the constraints of the present and the heat of the desert.

A line of poplars appears suddenly to the right of the road, a crystal channel of water running alongside. '*Karez*,' says Abdurrahman. 'It's water from the mountains.'

We get out to inspect the stream. The water is ice-cold. We take off our hot shoes and wade gratefully across. A few members of a *karez* commune come forward to meet us. Three naked children splash about in the stream and pause to greet us with 'bye-byes' of great vigour and friendliness. They have met foreigners before.

As we look upstream, the channel cuts more and more deeply into the desert, and finally disappears underground into what appears to be a cave. This is in fact a narrow tunnel, or *karez*, part of a system of tunnels that brings water down to Turfan from the mountains to the north. A *karez* is usually less than ten kilometres long, but some are as long as forty kilometres. The same volume of water flows all the year round; there is little depletion in summer, even with temperatures of as much as 48°C. All this is explained by Abdurrahman with a note of justifiable pride; within China, the *karez* is unique to Xinjiang.

'What if the roof caves in somewhere?' I inquire.

'The *karez* can be repaired.'

'Repaired?' I ask.

Abdurrahman smiles indulgently. 'After all, it was built once.'

'But there doesn't appear to be anywhere to get in from apart from the mouth. What if damage occurs a good distance inside – say, a few kilometres?'

Abdurrahman points to a slight rise in the ground. 'We can't see it from here, but there's an entrance there too. It's a hole, like the entrance to a well. It's fifty metres upstream, and there are entrances of that kind all the way along the *karez*. Some are further apart, but you can always get to the damage and repair it.'

We walk over to the opening and I am intrigued. The stream gurgles about three metres below, its surface almost unruffled. 'This,' says Abdurrahman, 'is where the *karez* commune members enter to maintain the channels. It's quite simple.'

The water is too tempting. 'I think I'll be an honorary commune member,' I murmur, as I take off my shoes, slip off my shirt and drop my legs over the edge of the well. 'See you at the mouth of the *karez*.'

Abdurrahman drops his avuncular air. 'No – no – ' he exclaims, 'there's nothing of interest inside. I wouldn't go down.' Then, yielding to the inevitable as I disappear downwards with a splash, he adds, 'Be careful!'

The walls are slippery, and I couldn't climb out even if I wanted to. There is not much light, which is something of a shock after the brilliant sunshine above. I notice how cold my feet are, and at first it feels comfortable. I walk slowly, groping along the slippery clay walls, bumping my head against the low roof. The light dies. I am guided solely by my hands and submerged feet, both suddenly numb with cold. There is a slight bend in the *karez*; I realise I had better feel the walls to make sure that there are no branches in the channel. It would be unpleasant to be lost here. The water washes up to my shorts, and when I speak aloud to myself my voice sounds hollow and garbled. Surely I must have gone more than fifty metres? In this unguided blackness the thought grips me that if the *karez* curves, it could still be a long way to the exit. Panic, I tell myself, is ridiculous – I can't be far from the mouth – and yet I feel it grow, so I talk myself forwards: a little further, a little further. Then there is another bend, a glimmer of light, then more light, and finally I run the last few steps into the lovely sunshine, chased, incidentally, by a small swarm of wasps whose nest I must have disturbed at the mouth of the *karez*.

I sit by the stream for a minute. There are more than two thousand kilometres of *karez* in the deserts of Xinjiang. Without them there would be no agriculture here, no grapes, melons or long-stapled cotton. Abdurrahman looks at me with relief, a little peeved with his ill-disciplined charge.

Greenery and flowing water: my father has always said that these form his idea of paradise. I would enjoy sitting here for a while, doing nothing in particular, but our guide is looking perturbedly at his watch. Almost everyone is back on the bus. 'Come along,' he says to me, 'we're going to see people buried in sand.'

This sounds inexplicable, if promising. We drive to a conical dune of dark sand. Umbrellas and tents protrude from its slopes, and people sit below, with their legs and sometimes their entire bodies submerged. They do not look unduly uncomfortable; some, indeed, appear relaxed, calm heads rising limbless like mushrooms from the sand. I take off my shoes for a better grip, and walk a few steps up the slope, only to run yelping down. As I nurse my scorched soles, I am told that the sand is not yet at its hottest. The best effect comes around two o'clock in the afternoon.

I have evidently missed part of the conversation. 'The best effect?' I ask, rubbing my traumatised feet.

'They do it to cure arthritis and other maladies,' says Abdurrahman with a gesture towards the dune. 'Why not go and have a picture of yourself taken sitting with them? Many of our foreign friends do.'

The status of a 'foreign friend' or 'foreign guest' in China is an interesting if unnatural one. Officialdom treats the foreigner as one would a valuable panda given to fits of mischief. On no account must any harm come to the animal. On the other hand, it must be closely watched at all times so that it does not see too much, do too much on its own, or influence the behaviour of the local inhabitants. 'We have friends all over the world,' announce banners slung up on the façades of hotels, but officialdom is disturbed by too much contact between Chinese and non-Chinese. They are horrified by affairs between Chinese and foreigners, especially if the woman is Chinese. From time to time this attitude bubbles over in tirades in the official press, but there is nothing like the xenophobia of the Cultural Revolution, when Beethoven was banned and diplomats beaten up by mobs.

As for the Chinese people, there is a general sense of friendliness and a curiosity towards the individual foreigner which is remarkable considering the anti-foreignness of the Chinese past, and indeed the stigma previously attached to contact with *waiguoren* (out-land persons). But the Chinese word for their country is simply 'Mid-land', an indication of their assumption of centrality in the scheme of things. One is often conscious of a minute examination of one's dress and behaviour upon first acquaintance; the impression is that one is considered not merely foreign, but in some sense weird. People passing one in the street stop to gape at dress and feature; on occasion even turning their heads round to stare and consequently bumping into bicycles or trees. Children yell, '*Waiguoren! waiguoren!*' as they catch sight of one; or, '*Waibin! waibin!*' (foreign guest) if they are old enough to combine etiquette with excitement.

> 'Papa, an Outlandman!' the toddler shrieks,
> Tugging his father's sleeve. 'Look, look,' he says,

> Gaping in shock at the unshaven cheeks,
> Long nose and camera and Outlandish ways.
> 'Look, look, a Midlandman,' I smile and say
> (In Midlandspeech). The toddler starts to cry.
> 'He spoke! He spoke! What is he anyway?'
> 'He is an Uncle,' is the sound reply.

Contact between Chinese and foreigners is permeated by the feeling that one's foreignness is the crucial element of one's character. With one's closest friends, however – and they are likely to be fairly knowledgeable about the world outside, or at least to be willing to conceive that Mid-land could be Out-land for Outlanders – one can share that acceptance, that tensionless and refreshing fellowship that makes one, through the enjoyment of their company, love the country from which they come.

One of the most unexpected features of my stay in Turfan is that it leads to my going to Tibet.

When I first came to China a year ago I wished to visit Tibet, but I soon put this idea aside as being impossible. The only people who obtain official stamps for Lhasa on their travel passes are wealthy groups of tourists whose programme is so carefully packed as to preclude the time for individual initiative or exploration. They pay about US $200 a day. Student friends, more eager than I to see Tibet, who were convinced that they could avoid the high prices, have tried to get their passes endorsed for Lhasa at a large number of police stations along the routes of their summer travels, but to no avail. I manage to get this permission because of two unlikely events: a song and a walk.

Late in the evening a troupe of local musicians perform a programme of songs and dances in the vine-covered courtyard of the guest house. We form a square under the trellis – the audience on three sides, the orchestra on the fourth, the dancers taking up the middle. It is wonderful to watch, and the music itself is beautiful, akin in spirit to that of the Middle East. Many of the songs are based on repartee between lovers – usually a tubby man with a wicked moustache and a woman with flashing eyes. Her manner consists in equal parts of affection and contempt. The orchestra yells out the chorus, rebuking this side, encouraging the other, commenting on the scene – or so I assume from their expressions, since I cannot understand the Uighur songs. The townspeople, who make up most of the audience, roll about in fits at the more outrageous verses.

When the troupe has performed, the townsfolk and musicians compel the foreign students to put on a show for them. A Japanese student plays the flute, the Italians sing revolutionary and feminist songs with their usual raucous aplomb. John Moffett, a lean and eccentric Englishman who talks like Bertie Wooster, interrupts his whimsical commentary on the proceedings to sing 'Ye Banks and Braes of Bonny Doon' in a pleasant and rich tenor.

It is now my turn to sing. There is no real choice. It will have to be the theme-song from *Awara* (*The Wanderer*), a sentimental Indian movie from the 1950s that is astonishingly popular in China. It comes as a shock to me sometimes to hear it hummed on the streets of Nanjing – to be transported without warning back to both India and childhood. No sooner have I begun than I find that the musicians have struck up the accompaniment behind me: they know the tune better than I do. The tubby man with the twirling moustaches is singing along with me, in Hindi at that. I am entranced, and, carried forward by their momentum, pour out the lyrics with abandon.

> 'No family, no world have I
> And nobody's love . . .'

I sing happily.

> 'Ah! My chest is covered with wounds.
> I am struck by the arrows of fate!'

When the song ends the orchestra and audience cheer me back to my seat. I am giddy with euphoria. This performance is to have certain repercussions the next day.

I would not normally have gone for a walk the next morning, but Claire is leaving the school trip for Nanjing, and later France. I know I will miss her good-natured company; I wander along with her to the market. She wants to buy a cap, and I a knife. The melons lie in huge heaps on the ground. A man brushes his teeth in the ditch by the side of the street. An old woman sits in a doorway reading a letter, occasionally fanning her face with it. Two soldiers go by, cracking sunflower seeds between their teeth.

We examine the wares of the pavement hawkers: dates and figs and grapes and vegetables as well as an assortment of clothes and shoes, utensils and other household goods. I buy something that looks like a crude wooden pipe from a Uighur woman, who holds up three fingers to indicate the price. It will make a good present for a smoker friend, I think, and on impulse buy two more, asking, in a mixture of Chinese and puffing gestures, whether I am holding it properly. The woman looks at me with incomprehension. A small crowd gathers, as it usually does around something as entertaining as a foreigner making a purchase, but there is an undercurrent of hilarity that I cannot fathom. Only later do I learn that the 'pipe' is a device for diverting a baby's urine out of its cot so that it does not soil its nightclothes.

Claire finds a cap that she likes, and I look at one in dark velvet with a bead design. I am about to go off in search of a knife when I notice a board in Chinese: Local Police Station. John and I have recently been discussing ways and means of getting to Tibet, so it is on my mind. I tell Claire I am going to try to have Lhasa stamped on my travel pass. She laughs with amiable scepticism and says she will see me at lunch. I enter the police station.

There is the kind of confusion within that could prove fertile: paper, files, maps, forms, and bilingual exchanges in loud voices. No one knows what to do with me. Finally a woman officer, kind and helpful beyond the call of duty, suggests that I follow her to the General Police Station, where they may be empowered to endorse passes; they certainly aren't at the local one. We walk halfway across town; the sun by now is unbearable. She is Han Chinese, has lived in Turfan for twenty years, speaks Uighur fluently, and has no fear of the heat; nevertheless she keeps telling me to walk in the spindly shade of the poplars lining the main street. At the General Police Station it is discovered that Akbar, the young officer who endorses travel passes, is not in. No one else can do it for him, as he has the key to the seals.

I sit down in the cool thick-walled corridor. Half an hour passes. Akbar finally enters with a friend of his. I am ushered into an office and asked what I have come for.

'I thought I would like to add a few more places to my travel pass,' I reply.

'Can I have a look at it?' I hand it over. 'You're from Nanjing, I see. Why didn't you get these places stamped at Nanjing?'

'Well, I would have liked to, but the Nanjing police were only willing to write sixteen places on the pass.'

'Sixteen?' Akbar looks surprised at the apparent arbitrariness of the number.

'There are four lines on the left-hand side of the page; they won't write more than four place-names on each line. They want things to look neat.' Akbar raises his eyebrows. 'In fact,' I continue, 'if one of your destinations has three or four characters in its name, you may be penalised for its length: they will then only fit three place-names on each line.'

Akbar allows himself a smile. 'I see. But they don't mind how many names are written on the facing page by another police station?'

'Oh no. That's for endorsements. When I asked them to continue the list on the right-hand page, they argued that the issuing station couldn't endorse itself.'

'Very logical,' says Akbar wryly. 'And where do you want to go?'

'Oh, I was thinking of going to Chengdu and Chongqing and Emei Shan and perhaps to Lhasa, and, oh yes, also to Wuhan and . . .'

'Well, write it all down on this form.' He gets one out from a drawer. When I have completed it he looks it over.

'And why do you want to go to Lhasa?' he homes in.

'I am interested in minority areas. I've always wanted to go, but I didn't think I'd have the time.' I examine a paper clip with interest.

'Please wait here. I may have to get permission from Urumqi – the provincial capital. This may take some time. I'm sorry for any delay.' He walks out with the form.

When he comes back half an hour later, he finds me and his friend deep in conversation about Indian movies. His friend was in the audience last night; we discuss *Awara* – its artistic merits and social significance. Because one of the themes of the movie is the question of whether 'a judge's son has to be a judge and a criminal's son a criminal', the movie was attacked during the Cultural Revolution, when pure proletarian antecedents were considered a guarantee of correctness of thought.

Akbar joins in the conversation. 'I hear that Lita died earlier this year.' (He is referring to Nargis, the actress who played the role of Rita.)

'What?' This is news to me. 'Where did you read this?'

'In a film magazine. I was very sorry to read about it. We take a lot of interest in Lita and Laz.' (Raj Kapoor, the director and leading actor.) 'Laz, it said in the magazine, is a big capitalist in real life, and has his own film company.' He says this with evident approval. Everyone I have ever talked to in China approves of Raj Kapoor. In fact he has a large body of fans in Russia and the Middle East as well.

The three of us talk in eccentric and exhilarating circles for another twenty minutes. Finally Akbar gets up.

'I think the telephone line to Urumqi is down. They've been having trouble with it recently. I doubt we can get through.' He pauses; I can see him swaying delicately towards a decision. 'Could you wait till tomorrow?' he asks, intending to defer it.

'We're leaving tomorrow,' I say, disappointed.

'Oh, well. Then I will endorse your pass now.' He goes to a cupboard, unlocks it and takes out the magic seal.

I can hardly believe my good luck. Outside in the searing sunshine I examine the inked characters and red official stamp on my travel pass. The endorsement is numbered '00001', and as it is already July, I conclude that the volume of endorsements through this police station cannot be excessive. As I walk back for lunch, a series of questions runs through my mind.

The first is whether I will avail myself of this endorsement for Lhasa. The problem is that I have already bought a ticket to go home via Hong Kong to Delhi. But could I go to Lhasa at any other time than now? In winter it will be dangerously cold in Tibet, and next summer I plan to leave China by the Trans-Siberian Railway. Besides, it is extremely unlikely that today's luck will ever repeat itself. The travel pass expires towards the end of August. It will have to be this summer or not at all – this summer that I had earmarked for exemplary and fulfilling laziness. And money: I could do with more of it. Why did I buy that ticket in advance? Can I get a refund later? But money, however much of a problem, is finally just money, and I know the answer to this question almost as soon as it forms.

The second question is how I should get to Lhasa. There is no railway. I will have to go by air from Xian or Chengdu. Which would be more convenient? Which will be cheaper? Or – and here an idea begins to germinate – would it be possible for me to go by road? Are there buses? Will the floods in western China have disrupted road traffic as they have rail traffic? Trucks? Jeeps? Surely there must be some way of getting to Tibet through its neighbouring provinces (Xinjiang, Qinghai, Sichuan and Yunnan)? It would certainly be cheaper than flying. Perhaps I could hitch-hike. The idea has the quality of a pleasant hallucination. I see before my eyes yaks, and trucks, and a huge image of the Potala palace. Two lamas stand in front of me and ask to see my travel pass. I hand them my air ticket from Hong Kong.

Back at the guest house, I spread out a map of China over my bed. There are, I discover, five ways of getting to Lhasa by road. One is from the west, via Kashgar – that is definitely out. Two others begin in Sichuan and Yunnan respectively; there is no immediately obvious reason for rejecting these. Finally, the remaining routes enter from the north: from Liuyuan in Gansu Province and from Xining in Qinghai Province; both of these converge on Germu (also in Qinghai). These look possible too, and have the additional advantage of crossing remote Qinghai, a province I have not seen.

Finally, a third question presents itself: after Lhasa, what? Should I return to Nanjing and then use my Hong Kong–Delhi air-ticket after all? Or should I try to continue overland to India? The border with India is disputed, and as an Indian citizen I am unlikely to get permission to cross it. But the border with Nepal may provide a possible exit route.

The answer to the previous question will predetermine the answer to a related one: before Lhasa, what? For if I decide to go directly from Lhasa to Kathmandu, I will need to return to Nanjing to get my passport, and from there go to Beijing to obtain a Nepalese visa before setting out for Lhasa. This is a depressing thought when I am already so close to the western routes that lead into Tibet. However, the prospect of crossing the Himalayas is sufficiently exciting to warrant the expense and tedium of this huge eastward loop.

I realise as I turn these thoughts over in my head that the chances of my getting through are very slight. I have not met anyone who has; I have heard of a number of foreigners who made it part of the way overland, only to be turned back by the police. But I do not know whether or not they had travel passes. The fact that I do certainly encourages me. I think it is worth a try.

After lunch (an exultant occasion: Claire is pleased and surprised by my documentary success) and a prolonged siesta (orchestrated by the buzz of flies and the whirr of an injured table-fan) we go off to see some more sights around Turfan – first the Grape Gorge, with its arbours and trellises and fast-flowing stone-lined canal. I threaten to swim in it, and Abdurrahman is disappointingly indifferent. 'Well, that's up to you,' he says. I look at the water for a while and realise that it is too dangerous. 'I think, after all, perhaps I won't take a swim.' Abdurrahman allows himself a fleeting smile and turns away.

Next comes the Emin Tower, a tall phallus of clay whose shifting shadow falls on the fields and roads around. We climb its spiral of narrowing steps for the fine view from the top. Graffiti (in both Chinese and Uighur) have been carved into the lattice-work on the uppermost windows. Finally we go to Turfan's museum, where we see all kinds of objects dating from the time when Turfan first became a halt along the Silk Route: strips of cloth, shards of ceramic, coins, toys, ornaments, stones. There is even a map of the Buddhist monk Fa Xian's fifth-century travels to India as well as one of Xuan Zang's journey two centuries later. I recall that Fa Xian mentions in his account that it is possible for a foreigner to travel from one end of India to another without a passport or pass of any kind; it is clear that the travel passes that foreigners in China inveigh against are not recent and exceptional impositions.

Throughout the afternoon a debilitating heat has drained our energy; even the will to think is draining away. Two or three times a day I wonder what I am doing in Turfan at all. The heat is poignantly described by my pictorial guide to Turfan:

Turpan's tourism is not very posperous but still, people come here to travel. The weather situation is unbearable since the temperature difference is really great. Turpan is also known as a 'Fire Place' in China. From the name, we can assume how hot the place is . . .

Turpan is so hot with daily temperatures of 40°C. The rocks, being heated by the sun, reach a temperature of 80°C. It is funny to see that people won't sweat since the sweat is evaporated before they come out to the outer layer of the skin.

But it is rather less funny to find oneself actually collapsing with heat-stroke. I wait until evening before wandering over to the market. Although this is a Muslim area, no women wear veils. A few children help their parents to load a donkey. Noticing my orange backpack they wave and shout the only foreign words they know: 'Bye-bye, bye-bye!' I return the greeting and turn to buy a couple of kilos of raisins and dates for future use. An old white-bearded man who has slung his bed over the pavement tells me to sit down. We talk for a while in Chinese over a glass of green tea. The talk drifts to the signs above the doors of shops around us. Apart from the Chinese characters, they are in the Latin and Arabic scripts.

'They're both Uighur,' says the old man.

'But I always thought Uighur was written in the Arabic scr.. ' I say.

'It was, when I learned to read and write. I can't read any of this Latin stuff.' He pauses. 'But the script was changed, and my son learned the Latin script.'

I sip my tea meditatively. 'It must be sad to know that your way of writing is dying out.'

'But it isn't. They changed the script back again. My grandson learns the Arabic script at school.'

'Oh! Why did they change the script the first time around?' I ask.

'I think the government was afraid that too many people were reading Russian publications in Uighur – which use the Arabic script. By changing to Latin, the Chinese government made sure that the new generation wouldn't understand the books that the Russians publish for their Uighur population.'

'And why did they change the script back to Arabic?'

'I don't know,' says the old man. 'It's the new Minorities Policy.' He reflects for a bit. 'The Latin script wasn't very successful. People didn't like it.'

'But some people learned only the Latin script, didn't they?' I think of Akbar, who could barely sign his name in the Arabic script. A horrific thought occurs to me. 'You and your grandson, then, can write notes or letters to each other, but your son can write to neither?'

'Quite right. That's how it is,' says the old man happily. The date-seller comes over to listen in, and a couple of men to look at my watch. As townsfolk gather around us out of curiosity, the old man stops talking and sips his tea. Someone recognises me from last night and I am coerced and cajoled into a repeat performance of the movie song. Then someone else – the son of the date-seller – sings a song in Uighur, then someone else again: the marketplace takes a spontaneous break for music. On my way back to the guest house, a young soldier gives me a lift on the back of his bicycle. I fear that I am taking him out of his way – and indeed I am – but he insists that I must be too tired to walk. This instinctive kindness is something one encounters every day in China.

I sit down by a bright bed of zinnias in the centre of the courtyard as evening falls, and watch their colours dim and merge. At night, under the grape trellis, a few of us foreigners sit and talk. John has left to travel further up the northwest railway line, to Urumqi. Since that is where we are bound for tomorrow, it is possible we will meet him. I like his unfettered manner of travelling; in spite of my congenital lethargy, I feel more than ever like breaking away from the guided comfort of the school trip.

As it is warm indoors, we pull our beds out and sleep under the vines, until, soon after dawn, the heat grows fierce again.

2

Heaven Lake

In the eastern provinces of China there is today little space for solitude or contemplation. In Nanjing, the city I live in for most of the year, there are Ming tombs outside the town itself, where, if I am willing to bicycle from the university, I can gain some sense of quiet: the wooded paths, with acorns and chestnuts strewn across the ground, the layers of leaf mould, the sunlight spraying through the branches of the *wutung* trees. The crowds visit the Ming tombs or the mausoleum of Sun Yat Sen, but the forest between these monuments, on the slopes of the Purple Gold Mountain (Zi jin shan) is deserted but for the occasional farmboy gathering acorns for fodder, the scratch and scamper of a squirrel ('pine-rat' in Chinese) or the startling chack of a magpie, an oversized version of its European counterpart. Here one can lie in the spring and autumn, and also in the summer, when the city-dwellers are gasping in the humid trap of the 'third furnace of the Yangtse' (the other two being Chongqing and Wuhan); the cooling canopy of leaves blunts the virulence of the heat.

Such refuges are rare in the eastern provinces, though, and their margins closely defined. The road, the observatory, the farms with their overpowering odour of pig manure, the well-visited historical monuments on either side of the wood, combine to curb the freedom of the wanderer. There are few places where poets like Tao Yuanming or Wang Wei would feel at ease today. Even where such still centres exist, more inaccessible perhaps, less amenable to blind construction and defacement, there are too many human impositions: calligraphy carved into a precipice as you turn a bend on a bamboo raft, or a red pavilion capping a peak of fern and pine.

But the western provinces are less oppressed by the charge of population and settlement. The day after we leave Turfan and arrive at Urumqi, I find an area of such natural beauty that I could live here, content, for a year. This is the region of Tian Chi, or Heaven Lake, a few hours by bus from Urumqi. It is not that this area is not geographically circumscribed (this time by desert rather than by tillage), but that its area is larger, so that one can wander for a day, for days, and not exhaust its limits. Again, it is not that man does not impinge on it, but that the unconscious ornamentation of hut and flock does not abrade its spirit or form.

It was initially John's idea to go to Heaven Lake. After we left Turfan, we discovered that he had forgotten to take with him his travel pass and residence permit – both essential documents. Since we too are heading for Urumqi, we bring them for him. When, after a short train journey, we arrive at the hotel there, we see him seated on the stone steps like one of the flanking lions at the entrance to buildings all over China, a disconsolate but anticipatory expression on his face. He cheers up considerably when he gets his pass back, and begins to talk about dinner. This is not the first important object that he has lost of late: he lost a pair of shoes earlier on in his travels – he left them behind on a train – and has since had to make do with slippers. There are even some who, having heard him apostrophising a mop as the head of Genghis Khan, believe that he has lost his mind. The two things that John seems incapable of losing are his good humour and his appetite. His continuing leanness complements a permanent hungry look. The large amounts of food he compresses inside himself are converted into a wiry energy remarkable in one so thin. After he cheerfully climbed Mount Emei in Sichuan in a few hours in midwinter ('trotted up' would be how he would put it), I began to wonder if he was immune to exhaustion in the way that some people are born physiologically immune to pain.

Dinner over, we return to our room and talk about travel plans. After visiting Heaven Lake, John plans to go further into Xinjiang. I discover that he met a Uighur family on the train to Xinjiang, who had adopted him, as indeed everyone who meets John is tempted to do. He responded by falling quickly and passionately in love with the daughter, another not infrequent occurrence. Now John wants to go to their home town, Kuche, yet further west. If he cannot get a pass, though, he will have to think of something else; he cannot jeopardise their good standing with the authorities by visiting them without permission. I mention that I now have a pass to Lhasa, and would much prefer hitch-hiking through western China to flying – if it is feasible. John also wants to go to Tibet; a policeman he has met on a train has offered him a possible lift from the railhead of Liuyuan all the way to Lhasa by jeep. Since Liuyuan, not far from here, is the starting-point for one of the routes that cross Qinghai, I ask if I can join him. John thinks it will be possible; this pleases me, as I have no idea how to set about getting a lift into Tibet and also because John would make, I think, an ideal travelling partner, with his practical manner and his sound core of madness.

Whilst in Urumqi, John mentions that he is interested in going to Heaven Lake, and, if he likes it, staying there for three or four days; for my part I am not eager to be shown further ruins by the local branch of the Foreign Affairs Office. The teachers from the university mention that they, too, will be making a day-trip to Heaven Lake, and describe the alternative delights on offer to the group: horse races and a visit to a Kazakh hut. But I am certain that I want to leave them for a few days, and in a little convulsion of flexibility, they agree.

The public bus from Urumqi to Heaven Lake leaves at eight the next morning; however, our hotel is a considerable distance outside the city, and there are no buses that could get us to the city centre in time. We stand on a deserted firing range at dawn, a forlorn knot of three – Ann, a friend of John's, is going to Heaven Lake for a day – gazing from the top of a mound at the long and trafficless road into town. Around seven o'clock we get a lift in a transport company truck, but this takes us just a couple of miles down the road. One further lift and a bus journey later we are in the city centre, but it is 8.05. Resigning ourselves to a day's delay, we decide not to go to the bus depot and instead to buy breakfast, when suddenly we see a bus with the sign 'Heaven Lake' bearing down on us. We try desperately to flag it down; the driver, catching sight of this unkempt trio, slams on the brakes.

We sit in the last row but one, bumped about but free of stares. The bus rolls out of the drab grid of the city, and we are soon in open countryside, with fields of sunflowers as far as the eye can see, their heads all facing us. Where there is no water, the land reverts to desert. While still on level ground we see in the distance the tall range of Mount Bogda, our destination, abrupt like a shining prism laid horizontally on the desert surface. It is over 5,000 metres high, and the peaks are under permanent snow, in powerful contrast to the flat desert all around. Heaven Lake lies part of the way up this range, about 2,000 metres above sea-level, at the foot of one of the higher snow-peaks.

As the bus climbs, the sky, brilliant before, grows overcast. I have brought nothing warm to wear; it is all down at the hotel in Urumqi. Rain begins to fall. The man behind me is eating overpoweringly smelly goats' cheese. The bus window leaks inhospitably but reveals a beautiful view. We have passed quickly from desert through arable land to pasture, and the ground is now green with grass, the slopes dark with pine. A few cattle drink at a clear stream flowing past moss-covered stones: it is a Constable landscape. The stream changes into a white torrent, and as we climb higher I wish more and more that I had brought with me something warmer than the pair of shorts that have served me so well in the desert. The stream (which, we are told, rises in Heaven Lake) disappears, and we continue our slow ascent. About noon we arrive at Heaven Lake, and look for a place to stay at the foot, which is the resort area. We get a room in a small cottage, and I am happy to note that there are thick quilts on the beds.

Standing outside the cottage we survey our surroundings. Heaven Lake is long, sardine-shaped and fed by snowmelt from a stream at its head. The lake is an intense blue, surrounded on all sides by green mountain walls, dotted with distant sheep. At the head of the lake, beyond the delta of the in-flowing stream, is a massive snow-capped peak which dominates the vista; it is part of a series of peaks that culminate, a little out of view, in Mount Bogda itself.

For those who live in the resort cottages there is a small mess-hall by the shore. We eat here sometimes, and sometimes buy food from the vendors outside, who sell kabab and *naan* until the last buses leave. The kababs, cooked on skewers over charcoal braziers, are particularly good;

highly spiced and well-done. Horses' milk is available too from the local Kazakh herdsmen, but I decline this. I am so affected by the cold that Mr Cao, the relaxed young man who runs the mess, lends me a spare pair of trousers, several sizes too large but more than comfortable. Once I am warm again, I feel a pre-dinner spurt of energy – dinner will be long in coming – and I ask him whether the lake is good for swimming in.

'Swimming?' Mr Cao says. 'You aren't thinking of swimming, are you?'

'I thought I might,' I confess. 'What's the water like?'

He doesn't answer me immediately, turning instead to examine some receipts with exaggerated interest.

I look at the water again, inviting and smooth, just begging a body to slice through it, to luxuriate in its clear depths. I untie my shoelaces. This little mess will serve as a changing room; after all, I have just changed into a pair of trousers here.

Mr Cao, with great offhandedness, addresses the air. 'People are often drowned here,' he says. After a pause, he continues. 'When was the last one?' This question is directed at the cook, who is preparing a tray of *mantou* (squat white steamed breadrolls), and who now appears, wiping his doughy hand across his forehead. 'Was it the Beijing athlete?' asks Mr Cao.

'Yes, yes, it was the Beijing athlete.'

'The Beijing athlete?' I quaver. The placidity of this water must be deceptive.

'Yes, I think so,' says Mr Cao to the cook. 'He'd swim across the lake and back every day . . .'

'Every day,' repeats the cook.

'And then one day he swam to the other side, and had just started on his way back when he simply disappeared. Drowned.'

'Drowned,' tolls the cook.

'Drowned? The Beijing athlete?' I ask, anxiously.

'Yes,' says Mr Cao. 'He was from an athletics college in Beijing. Or was it Tianjin?'

'Beijing,' says the cook, with authority.

'But . . . how did this happen?' I blurt out.

Mr Cao has gone back to his receipts. He looks up at the cook, who says, in a lugubrious tone, 'Well, no one knows. He might have had a heart attack.'

'Or he might have got cramp,' suggests Mr Cao.

'Or maybe the water was too cold,' adds the cook.

'Or maybe it was a current under the surface. No one knows. His body was never found.'

'Never found,' mutters the cook as he heads back for the kitchen.

I retie my shoelaces.

Later, however, temptation overcomes caution; I take a short dip, keeping close to the shore. The water is clean and extremely cold, and I splash around for a few minutes before emerging blue and refreshed. John and I walk around the foot of the lake looking for the point where it flows out into the stream that we drove along this morning. We find it, eventually, and it is spectacular, the more so since the sky is now in the last multicoloured spasms of sunset. The stream plunges downwards in a series of cataracts through the pines, into a small round blue pool, almost completely enclosed by forested slopes. The pool is probably about thirty metres across; the stream that we assume must flow out from it cannot be seen – which is odd, because the whole pool seems to be visible.

We spend several days at Heaven Lake wandering around, though John's slippers severely hinder him. The day John is leaving, we go down to the small ice-blue serendipitous pool with a picnic lunch provided by Mr Cao (bread, dry cooked meat, peanuts, tomatoes and oranges). We are completely cut off from the world. It drizzles and is brilliantly sunny by turns. We make a fire in the lee of a rock, swim nude without fear of upsetting chance tourists, sun ourselves or shiver before the fire as the weather alternates, eat, drink and are merry. The pool, it seems, flows out in one hammering vertical plunge through a narrow slit in its steep enclosing walls, then churns through a sluice of rock into a gorge-like stream bed. It is this stream that we saw tamely channelled through pasture and field a few miles below, finally disappearing into the sand and heat of the desert around.

John leaves ('trundles along', in his phrase) by the afternoon bus. We have agreed to meet in about two weeks to begin our journey to Tibet. I will miss his Monty Python banter which exaggerates (and thus defuses) the irritations and inefficiencies of travelling. When I get back to our room I find that he has left a dictionary behind.

I decide to stay an extra day or two at Heaven Lake, so much do I like this place. I spend them roaming around by the head of the lake, watching herdsmen cross the stream delta with cattle and horses; walking towards the snowline; or reading Confucius' *Analects*. I lie on a rock by the shore, and read very slowly, pausing to digest it with segments of orange. I find the sage himself somewhat stodgy until, among the strictures and dicta, the condemnations of improprieties and impieties, I come across a passage where he is talking to his disciples:

When Tzu-lu, Tseng Hsi, Jan Yu and Kung-hsi Hua were seated in attendance, the Master said, 'Do not feel constrained simply because I am a little older than you are. Now you are in the habit of saying, "My abilities are not appreciated," but if someone did appreciate your abilities, do tell me how you would go about things.'

Tzu-lu promptly answered, 'If I were to administer a state of a thousand chariots, situated between powerful neighbours, troubled by armed invasions and by repeated famines, I could, within three years, give the people courage and a sense of direction.'

The Master smiled at him.

'Ch'iu, what about you?'

'If I were to administer an area measuring sixty or seventy *li* square, or even fifty or sixty *li* square, I could, within three years, bring the size of the population up to an adequate level. As to the rites and music, I would leave that to abler gentlemen.'

'Ch'ih, how about you?'

'I do not say that I have the ability, but I am ready to learn. On ceremonial occasions in the ancestral temple or in diplomatic gatherings, I should like to assist as a minor official in charge of protocol, properly dressed in my ceremonial cap and robes.'

'Tien, how about you?'

After a few dying notes came the final chord, and then he stood up from his lute. 'I differ from the other three in my choice.'

The Master said, 'What harm is there in that? After all, each man is stating what he has set his heart upon.'

'In late spring, after the spring clothes have been newly made, I should like, together with five or six adults and six or seven boys, to go bathing in the River Yi and enjoy the breeze on the Rain Altar, and then go home chanting poetry.'

The Master sighed and said, 'I am all in favour of Tien.'

I walk back along the shore by boulders and juniper bushes. The round Kazakh tents squat at the head of the valley in a grassy clearing among pines. Pieces of driftwood lie among the pebbles on the shore. In places, a white cottony blossom lies thickly on the ground, making it slippery underfoot. It is now drizzling.

At the resort area I find that the Nanjing University group has come to Heaven Lake for a few hours. We return together to Urumqi. The next morning we are given an hour or so of 'free activity' before we board the train eastwards. I am walking briskly towards the Urumqi mosque when I notice a pedlar selling sheepskin jackets on the pavement. He glances quickly at my shoes to confirm that I am a foreigner, and doubles the price I have just heard him offer to a passer-by. We haggle for a few minutes until I bring out some 'funny money' (foreign exchange certificates denominated in Chinese currency, issued to foreigners in lieu of ordinary currency by the Bank of China); then his eyes glow with interest and I am able to get a good deal on the purchase. He, too, is satisfied, for with these certificates he can buy fancy goods in the so-called 'Friendship Stores' – goods that are more expensive, and sometimes unavailable, elsewhere.

I am still hurrying to the mosque when a dark, narrow shop, with caps of all kinds displayed by its doorway, catches my eye. I stop: I will need a cap to protect myself in Tibet from the rays of the sun. The interior of the shop is dingy. A sewing machine is clattering anciently away. Moons of cloth, strips of plastic, bobbins of thread, circles of cardboard lie on the floor, or on shelves, or hang from nails in the door. An old, bespectacled, bearded man, sharp-featured and dark, sits inside the shop talking in Uighur to a boy of about twelve. When I enter, he addresses me in Uighur. I shrug my shoulders. He repeats his sentence, but louder this time.

'I don't understand,' I say in Chinese.

He understands this, but not much more, in Chinese. 'Hussain!' he calls out in a thin and authoritarian voice.

Hussain, who must have learned Chinese at school, asks me what I want.

'A cap. Maybe one of those.' I say, pointing at blue cloth caps hanging by the door. 'How much are these?'

The boy speaks to the old man, who holds up three fingers.

'Three yuan. Are you travelling through here? Where are you from?'

'Yes,' I answer, as I try on a couple for size. 'I'm from India. This one fits. I'll buy this one.' I take out a five yuan note.

'Yindu!' exclaims the boy. He exchanges a few excited words with the old man, who peers at me over his spectacles in annoyed disbelief. The boy runs out of the shop.

'Yes, Yindu. Hindustan,' I say, hoping to convince the old man. In a flash of inspiration, I pull out my pen and write 'Hindustan' on the palm of my hand, in Urdu.

The old man readjusts his spectacles, catches hold of my wrist tightly and peers at the writing. Urdu and Uighur share the Arabic script; as he reads it his face lights up.

'Ah, Hindustan! Hindustan!' This is followed by a smiling salvo of Uighur. He hands me three yuan in change.

'But the cap costs three yuan,' I say, handing him back the extra yuan, and raising three fingers.

He refuses to take it, and I refuse to do him out of a yuan. Suddenly, with an exasperated gesture, he grabs the cap from off my head and begins to rip it apart. I am horrified. What is he doing? What have I done? Have I insulted him by refusing his gift? Fifteen young boys suddenly appear at the door with Hussain at their head. They gather at the open entrance in a jigsaw of heads and gaze unblinkingly at the man from India. They are all speaking at once, and I am even more concerned and confused than before.

The old man shouts 'Hussain!' There is silence in the shop. He then fires rapid sentences off at me, which the boy translates.

'My father says he will make the stitching firmer for you because you will be travelling a long way.'

With a few strong pulls of the needle and a few minutes at the sewing machine, the old man, now intent on his work and paying me not the slightest attention, stretches and stitches the cap into a tougher form. With a restrained smile, and a faint snort of satisfaction, he stands up to put it back on my head, gently, and adjusts it to the correct angle. He says a few more words, but I am too moved by his kindness to think of asking Hussain for a translation. As I nudge past the fifteen spectators at the door, I turn to say 'salaam aleikum', knowing that he will understand this.

He repeats the words, and I walk back into the street.

I have rejoined the school trip; our next journey is by train to Xian. The train eastwards is leaving soon. I get on, having decided to return for a short while to Nanjing and Beijing in order to complete formalities, to pack appropriately for the journey to Tibet, and to see Xian, the ancient capital of China. There is some frustration in all this. I could see Xian next year; but a passport, a Nepalese visa, a cell for the light-meter of my camera and money for further travel force me to make this eastward diversion. As the train passes through Liuyuan I chew a little helplessly over the fact that I will be travelling for more than a week, merely to return to this point in order to continue my journey south.

3

An eastward loop

Xian reminds me irresistibly of Delhi. It is, I think, the broad streets, the dryness, the shop-fronts with their small canopies leaning out over the pavements, the bicycle-riding white-shirted population – it is too hot to wear the otherwise ubiquitous thin blue cotton jackets – and, most of all, the city wall, the presence of history. The only other place where I have had a similar sense of *déjà vu* is Shanghai. There the intolerable density of population, the sluggish river crammed with boats and sewage, and the vestiges of British commercial architecture combine to create an atmosphere evocative of Calcutta. Beijing and Nanjing, the two cities I know best, remind me of nothing but themselves.

Xian lies on the site of Changan, the capital of China during one of the most brilliant of its periodic flourishings of culture. There is almost too much to see here, and since I have rejoined the group, I see it all: museums, including the 'forest of steles', one of the most famous collections of calligraphic inscriptions; sites of prehistoric settlements; the pool where the emperor Ming Huang first set eyes on Yang Gui Fei, the courtesan who disrupted the Tang empire and cost him his throne; the site of the tomb of the Empress Wu in the dry hills a few hours outside the city; but, most remarkable of all, the vast underground labyrinth where Qin Shi Huang was buried, with its thousands of soldiers and horses, life-size in clay, testimony to the megalomania of the first great unifier of China, and to the skill of artisans over two thousand years ago.

I should have known that this hectic tourism would inevitably exhaust me. One evening, in search of a haven among the bus horns and bicycle bells, I walk through a maze of alleys to the Grand Mosque of Xian. It is late, almost the time for prayer, and I stand outside the entrance to the first courtyard until the gatekeeper roughly asks me what I want. There follows a short and aggressive interrogation, after which I am allowed into the courtyard. I sit and watch the white-capped, white-clad believers pass through a gateway into the second courtyard, and from there into the eaved prayer-hall. The imam, also in a white turban, has a word or two with the man watching the gate before he goes in to lead the prayers.

I sit in the courtyard, imbibing the evening calm, the beauty of the place. There is a pomegranate tree, a small pavilion, a few stone tablets with Chinese and Arabic inscriptions. Arabic inscriptions cover the entranceways into the courtyards, and on the platform where the main hall stands are ceramic basins filled with mossy stones.

When the service is over, I walk to the entrance of the main hall. It is of an austere simplicity; the one concession to comfort is a large threadbare rug spread over the floor. I do not enter, as a few worshippers are still on their knees inside.

A casually dressed young man with a high-boned, sensitive face approaches me while I'm still standing under the eaves. 'Excuse me, which country are you from?' he asks, hesitantly.

'India.'

'I saw you wandering about the courtyards. I felt a bit embarrassed about the way the gatekeeper treated you.'

'Oh, that was nothing.'

'He's a bit abrupt, that's all.'

'Yes. I wasn't annoyed. This is a beautiful mosque.'

'You know, I've been watching you for a while, while you've been taking photographs. You have a very respectful attitude.'

I burst out laughing. 'Really? Well, really, I didn't think . . . This is such a beautiful place; peaceful, calm. Do you work here?'

'No, not yet. I'm learning Arabic from one of the imams.'

'This place is interesting – half Arabic in style, half Chinese. The inscriptions too, some in Chinese, some in Arabic. That, for instance,' I say, pointing to the inscription across an arch, 'you could find in any mosque in the world. But this,' I gesture towards the small pavilions in the courtyard, 'you wouldn't see outside China.'

On the arch, carved in Arabic, is the fundamental credo of Islam: 'There is no God but God, and Mohammed is his prophet.' The first half of the inscription is especially striking, with its repeated vertical strokes of '*laam*' and '*alif*'. 'Can you read Arabic?' asks the young man. 'Are you Muslim?'

'Well, I can read the script, very slowly, but I don't understand the language. I only know what that means because I've seen it so often before. And I'm not Muslim. But one tenth of the people of India are, and some of our languages use that script.'

By now it is almost dark. We stroll towards the deserted courtyard where repairs are going on. 'What happened to this place during the Cultural Revolution? The mosques in Nanjing, I know, were closed down. In some places the imams were sent to prison.'

He looks uncomfortable. 'This place, too, was closed down and fell into disrepair. We've re-opened sections of it just recently.'

'Was there any destruction?'

'Yes, there was some. This part of the city is Muslim, though, and the lanes are narrow. The people banded together, and prevented the Red Guards from doing much harm.'

'But did services continue at all during that period?'

'No. The imams were ordered not to hold services.'

I decide not to ask any more questions; we carry on walking. He talks about the wall structure and Chinese roofs, comments on the absence of cupolas. Suddenly he turns towards me and says, 'There were some services. But they were in private homes. You know, that is where women normally pray, at home. So it was not so difficult to arrange things, though of course they had to be held secretly. The whole flavour of our life changed during those years. We could hardly even eat meat, because none of the meat sold in the shops had been slaughtered in the prescribed manner. It was considered a vestige of feudal thought for us to maintain the custom.'

'Things are better now, I suppose?'

'Yes, better. But once something like that has happened . . . No, it's better now. Maybe it'll stay this way.'

We talk for a while of interesting but more neutral matters, and he asks me to have dinner at his house. I would greatly like to, but I already have a dinner appointment.

'When do you leave Xian?' he asks.

'Tomorrow.'

'If you're in Xian again . . .'

'I'll ask for you at the mosque.'

'No. Let me give you my address.' The young man scribbles on the back of an old bus ticket. He waits at the bus stop with me – I tell him it's not necessary, but he smiles it off – until the bus comes. Later I discover that my dinner date has been called off. I feel a pang of regret that I had not spent the evening in the congenial company that had been offered to me with so much openness and goodwill.

Returning to Nanjing has for me the flavour of a minor homecoming: my room, my friends, familiar sights. But the moist heat of the city, which even the trees lining the main roads barely lessen, is conducive to stupor rather than to carrying out the enormous number of errands I have to cram into one day. I rummage about my room for my passport, a few clothes, three or four books; cadge a new cell for my camera's light-meter from a friend; cash a cheque for a few hundred yuan; buy a ticket for Beijing; and examine my mail.

Everyone who returns after an absence of a month to the place where he lives, knows, as he opens his mailbox, a uniquely bitter-sweet mixture of anticipation and apprehension. There is no letter from Stanford about my research, but then there are no unpaid bills either. At least my family has not forgotten me. I read their letter with a twinge of conscience: they are expecting me to be home by the 25th of August, on a flight from Hong Kong. I write a cryptic note, saying that I'm going to try to return 'by a more interesting route'. I cannot say more, since it is an open secret that foreigners' mail is read in China. I hope that they will not be too worried if I am not on the scheduled plane. I mention that I will be home by the end of August at the latest.

For all the enthusiasm with which I am undertaking this journey, I am conscious that I know almost nothing about Tibet. My understanding of what I see will lack the counterpoint of expectation, of a previous comprehension, however fragmentary. I have always wanted to go to Tibet, yet I know that this is largely due to the glamour surrounding the unknown. About Tibetan religion I know very little; and I will have to learn about the climate and geography at first hand. I have no Tibetan friends. A picture of the Potala, Tibetan dancers seen in Darjeeling, an article or two in the newspapers about the Dalai Lama, chance remarks made since my childhood: it is of scraps such as these that my idea of Tibet is composed. And in one sense my purpose is not to travel in Tibet, but merely to pass through it: 'coming home', as I write to my parents, 'by a more interesting route.'

Perhaps, I tell myself, this journey will be wasted on me unless I make a concentrated effort to read about Tibet. I envisage a crash course on the subject: a book on Tibetan history, one on Tibetan religion, a reading of the relevant section of Nagel's *Encyclopaedia-Guide: China*. But books, even if I were able to obtain them here, are heavy to carry, and it is too late to sit down and read them. Time has become an important constraint. Besides, I tell myself optimistically, the freshness of the vision may compensate for the ignorance of the viewer. I have only one day in Nanjing and a lot to do. I can't spend the time hunting for books. The few paperbacks I pack are those I have wanted to read during my year in China but have not read for lack of time. They include the *Lao Tzu* and the *Chuang Tzu*: Chinese, not Tibetan, classics.

I continue packing. Sleeping bag? Too bulky, I decide. My small orange backpack? It could be useful; if I don't need it I can easily pack it away into another bag. A few research materials? Yes, I can look them over when I get to India. It occurs to me that my spectacles are badly scratched. I decide to get a new pair, in case my present ones get lost or deteriorate any further. Time is probably too short now, but in any case I can try. My bike has a puncture, and I realise with a pang that I will have to make the sweaty journey to the opticians on foot. By the time I get there I am in a kind of a daze.

> Below the broadleafed planes the sweltering street
> Contorts and shimmers in the miraging heat

33

That like a melting lens now damps now swells
The shrill cicada-choir of bicycle bells.

The kindly old man in charge of the shop gives me a glass of water and a fifteen-minute eye-test. I am lucky; the vision is the same in both eyes, and a pair of ready-made spectacles is in standard stock. He moulds the frame over a candle and fits it to my face again and again until he is satisfied. The whole thing comes to less than 10 yuan, including thirty cents for the test. (A yuan is a little more than half a US dollar.) Elated by how pleasantly and quickly all this has gone, I walk out into the concussive heat of the street.

It is my last evening in Nanjing, and I go out with Claire – she has not yet left for France – to the Shuang Men Lou Hotel for dinner. I wear Chinese clothes, as I have during much of the summer, but now that I have had my hair cut and have Chinese spectacles, the guard at the gate challenges me.

'Stop, comrade.'

I keep on walking. He runs up to me and holds me by the shoulder. 'Didn't you hear me? What unit are you from? You can't go in there.' It is dark, so he cannot see my features too well. Claire walks up to me, and we smile. The guard looks abashed, but I am pleased that with my loss of hair and gain of spectacles I do not now appear too emphatically un-Chinese. If I need to stress my foreignness I will fiddle with the knobs on my digital watch.

For this last supper in Nanjing I have bought a bottle of Californian red wine at the Friendship Store: Paul Masson's Rubion, incomparably better than the second-rate French, Spanish and Italian wines of similar price available there. But the price has just gone up and, disgruntled, I go on to expatiate on the increased demand for wine, general inflation, yuan-dollar exchange-rates and mark-up percentages for luxury goods. Claire looks on with a bemused expression and probably wonders why I have bought the bottle at all. But it all seems worthwhile as we drink the lovely well-analysed liquid. Nostalgia for the Golden State, and particularly San Francisco, pours over me in pacific waves, and even Claire, through the mesh of her French loyalties, admits that perhaps the Californians can produce wines after a fashion.

Increasingly of late, and particularly when I drink, I find my thoughts drawn into the past rather than impelled into the future. I recall drinking sherry in California and dreaming of my earlier students days in England, where I ate *dalmoth* and dreamed of Delhi. What is the purpose, I wonder, of all this restlessness? I sometimes seem to myself to wander around the world merely accumulating material for future nostalgias.

I have been to Beijing twice before; once in the October cold when the hills near the Great Wall were covered with the reds of autumn, and once in the spring when there were violent dust storms; but this time it is just as much of a furnace as Nanjing. I enjoy a leisurely two days there. One of my friends tells me that what I propose to do is 'a damn foolish idea, Jesus, you must be mad,' but most of them are encouraging if pessimistic about my chances of getting through to Lhasa. The main purpose of my visit to Beijing is to get a visa for Nepal. The Nepalese Embassy tells me that Indian citizens do not require a visa for Nepal. The only document I will need in order to leave China is an exit visa; this I already have, and it specifies no particular place of exit. I convince myself that to exit from Tibet will be just as valid as to fly out from Shanghai. I am to discover that I am wrong.

When I set out from Beijing for Lanzhou I feel a surge of optimism, despite the gloomy predictions of my friends. At last I am moving back towards the deserts of the northwest. The best way to preserve this mood is not to think more than a couple of days ahead. As for the trip to Lhasa, there is John's friend, the policeman, and if that doesn't work out, something else, I tell myself, is bound to turn up.

The journey to Lanzhou is by train, first diesel and then steam. The route runs along the Great Wall, then the northern grasslands, and finally along the Yellow River, the railway line hugging the wall of hill above. It is pleasant to be travelling by myself. I can stare out of the window for hours, watching the river turn silver towards evening, and the green irrigated corridor surrounding it grow narrower as we move up-river. Or I can talk to my fellow-travellers, many of whom will never have met a foreigner before. Once you get past the inevitable questions (nationality, age, occupation, salary, cost of watch, what do you think of China, etc.), conversations broaden out into more interesting channels: politics, art, the recent floods, Sino–Indian relations, the price of watermelons in different places. Discussions meander on as station follows station, interrupted only by meals and broadcasts on the loud-speakers. In general, unless you are talking to a political cadre, people show a frankness and a curiosity that I had not expected when I first came to China. Train journeys are the best of all. Chinese rarely get to travel – apart from Sundays, workers get only eight days off in the year – and there is usually a sense of euphoria in escaping from one's work-unit, if only for a short time. Besides, a conversation with a foreigner whom you will probably never see again triggers no signal for caution. Finally, it is true that the Chinese policy towards foreigners is very slowly, if irregularly, becoming more liberal.

I say irregularly, because from time to time the *People's Daily* thunders out against the corrupting influence of foreigners, their music and clothes and sexual morality, their lack of seriousness and their exploita-tive intentions. China is to learn foreign science and technology, not foreign habits and mores. But contact cannot be as aseptic as all that. The Chinese students in the US, Canada, Japan and Europe – and there are thousands of them – will not return home unaffected by their general experiences. Nor will foreign students in China refrain from contact with their Chinese classmates. The lapses into paranoia that the official line sometimes suffers from, and that universities have to follow, cannot but harm the much-acclaimed cause of international friendship. One's attitudes towards a place are only partly determined by the greatness of its history, or the magnificence of its scenery. When I think of China, I think first of my friends and only then of Qin Shi Huang's tomb.

Lanzhou is a brown-earthed dreary city stretched out along the upper course of the Yellow River. I buy some travel-sickness pills, repair my watch-strap, and get a small black travelling bag to go with my Chinese clothes and spectacles. I take a bus for a few stops, hoping to see something of interest in Lanzhou, but give it up as pointless: 'There is no there there.'

But Lanzhou merely embodies more completely what is present to a greater or lesser degree in all Chinese cities: a stupefying architectural sameness, based on a stupefyingly ugly set of models. Street of standard shop-cuboid follows street of standard shop-cuboid. There is no basic variation in the design of workers' flats, government offices, parks, bookstores or even streetlamps. The difference in street architecture between, say, Beijing and Guangzhou (Canton) is far less marked than the difference in climate would lead one to expect. In the countryside, as one passes by train from province to province, sometimes even from county to county, the houses change: the building materials, the shape of the doorways, the eaves of the roofs, the style of the walls and courtyards, the number of windows, everything changes along with climate and terrain.

But this harmony with nature is absent in the stodgy and conformist architecture of the cities. (Even the names of streets repeat themselves from city to city; the bookstores all have the same name and there is invariably a Sun Yat Sen Park to visit.) However, the older parts of the cities, the lanes and alleys, are their one saving grace: here the style varies both among and within cities, as concessions are made to climate and individual taste.

Almost all modern construction is undertaken by the government: it requires much less thought and expense if the same designs can be implemented everywhere. To be innovative or individual or eccentric is to risk criticism.

Nor is it just in architecture that this monotony makes itself felt. The clothes people wear are similar in style and colour (deep blue, and greens and greys). There is little contrast or brightness to meet the eye as one looks down the street. And in the evening everything closes down by eight o'clock. With the exception of a few all-night eateries intended for night-shift workers, and – recently – one or two catering to the foreign tourist trade, you cannot get a meal in a restaurant after 6.30 pm. At night, a pall of tedium settles over the city. Almost everyone is at home, and has to get up at six o'clock in the morning to go to work.

Some cities do show a few signs of individualism: the tea and coffee shops of Kunming, the gardens of Suzhou, Xian's great city wall, or the plane trees of Nanjing compensate to some extent for the identicality of their main streets. Moreover, it is only in the cities that one will find good restaurants, movie theatres, playhouses, exhibitions and museums. But for all this, the first impression one gets is of a wearisome physical predictability; and Lanzhou is a paradigm of this unloveliness.

John is staying at the Lanzhou Hotel. He has shaved off all his hair against the heat, and looks worn out. He has been unwell since we last met – mainly stomach troubles and exhaustion. He was not able to get permission to go to Kuche, and has spent the last week in Urumqi. He is clearly too tired to try for Tibet; he plans now to continue on to Loyang, and from there to Hong Kong and eventually England. I return his dictionary to him. We talk late into the night and the following day share a parting apple. Though it is clear that he has made the right decision, I am filled with a sense of regret.

As I am about to board the train for Liuyuan, my final destination by rail, I feel a hand on my shoulder. I turn around to face a middle-aged depressed-looking man with a wheedling voice. He asks me a number of questions in an interrogatory manner, and from the way the platform attendants defer to him, I assume that he is a plainclothes policeman. After an officious, offensive and unhurried examination of my travel pass, interspersed with insinuating and adenoidal queries, he lets me onto the train only seconds before it is due to pull out.

I am upset, but say nothing as I clamber into the carriage. My luggage is pushed on after me. A young man sitting opposite me, who has watched this scene, offers me a cigarette. He lights up himself, then offers his pack around to the other travellers near us. I don't usually smoke – I smoked perhaps one cigarette a year before I came to China – but I have learned in the villages where I carried out my research that a cigarette refused may be taken as a slight. In fact, a 555 or a Kent, exchanged for a Peacock or a Double Happiness, is a quick way to break the ice with people you have just met. At one time I was smoking, with no enjoyment and with some discomfort, more than a pack a day. The Chinese smoke more than any other people I have met; the men, that is: it is not considered appropriate for a woman to enjoy a cigarette; dissolute women in movies may be identified by their inexpert but determined puffing.

The young man is an engineer, one of a group of engineers and technicians who are on their way to install some radio equipment near the Soviet border. We talk, share food, play cards. The carriage contains travellers of different nationalities: Han, Uighur, Kazakh, Mongolian. There are young people, returning resentfully to their far-flung outposts after a rare visit home to Shanghai. 'We have been sent to New Zealand for life,' says one bitter young man. 'We could just as well be on the moon.' 'New Zealand' or Xin-xi-lan, is an acronym for Xin-jiang, Xi-zang (Tibet) and Lan-zhou. To be posted to any of these places, is, for most Han people, to be condemned to an uncomfortable and barbarous limbo.

Two members of a women's tennis team, returning to Urumqi after a successful tournament in Beijing, take out a pack of cards and give the men a drubbing. An older woman talks about the grain supply organisation she works for, and about the drought and near-famine which have struck large parts of China this year. Counterpointing her story, rain comes down in sheets outside the window, and the semi-desert ravines swirl with the waters of a flash-flood. As the train jolts on, her six-year-old son draws our attention to the more spectacular torrents, and tells me to take photographs, laughing half gleefully half ruefully whenever a tree or telegraph pole ruins my shot. His mother warns him not to 'disturb Uncle'.

My camera is examined – it is a Nikon on which I spent the last of my savings – and disappointment expressed when it is discovered that it is not a Polaroid. All foreigners are expected to have cameras that develop photographs instantly. My watch, a present from my father after two watchless years, and full of superfluous gimmickry – chime, stopwatch, alarm, etc. – is passed from hand to hand and much admired. I am asked whether I have 'established house', i.e. got married yet, and anxiety is expressed when I say that, although I'm twenty-nine, I haven't. My family photograph is taken out, and I am asked to explain my mother's *tika* and my father's *kurta*, not to mention my sister's cut-off jeans. It is decided that the 1962 border conflict between India and China was 'just an unfortunate incident, the fault of governments, not of peoples, and anyway a very short period of hostility when looked at in the perspective of such a long friendship.' The Russians are denounced, Raj Kapoor praised, the trial of the Gang of Four cautiously skirted around, the government system of job allocation debated. What job will I be allocated when I return home? When I tell them that I will look for one myself, this arouses a good deal of amazement and interest. When I critically examine the Indian birth control programme, I am asked, with some incredulity, how I can possibly criticise my country's official line.

I spend a comfortable night on the middle bunk (Chinese sleepers are three-tiered in the 'hard sleeper' class), and wake up to the strains of radio music blaring out on the loudspeaker system. This is one of the banes of railway travel in China. In general, however, train journeys are comfortable compared to those in India, and one is provided with a continuous supply of drinkable hot water, which the Chinese imbibe in extraordinary quantities, with or without tea.

At five in the afternoon of the second day, the train stops at Liuyuan, which is as far as it will take me in the direction I want to go. I get off and look around. Liuyuan is a dusty, treeless, godforsaken depot, its main street merging with the road to Lhasa, now 1,800 kilometres away. But as I look down the empty street, it comes home to me that I don't have the faintest idea about how to get a lift. Enquiries reveal that the possible contact John had mentioned is nowhere to be found.

4

Liuyuan:

of trucks and tribulations

I fix myself up in a local hotel with the simplest of facilities: a bed, a wash-basin. There is no running water, but it's cheap: two yuan a night. Outside the room is a yard where nothing grows. Nothing grows anywhere in Liuyuan.

I leave my luggage in my room and, despite the fact that the window cannot be shut, I close the door carefully and lock it. I am meticulous when I am at a loss. I walk out onto the street to think about the next step.

The name Liuyuan means Willow Garden, but there is not a tree around. A dusty terminus for truck traffic, it marks the start of the road south to Tibet. Much of what goes into Tibet from eastern China is unloaded in Liuyuan's vast railroad yard, and then reloaded onto trucks bound southwards. From Liuyuan the trucks travel to Germu in the province of Qinghai, and from there to Lhasa. Oil from the northeast, machinery from Shanghai, materials and chemicals, shoes, clothing, toys; many of the industrial products that Tibet needs are taken in through her neighbouring provinces, along roads built since the Chinese entry into Tibet in 1959.

The main street of Liuyuan is like the set of a small town Western: broad, brown, dusty, with a few stores and eating places strung out along the sides of the street. However, it is a camel-cart that is parked outside the bank. Wires grid the sky. A few cobblers and tailors sit outside the foodstore with their machines, looking desultorily at the dust that is whirling about in a sudden wind. From time to time a truck comes growling down the street from the direction of the railway station. A man, face strained with effort, pulls a large cartload of coal past a slogan-splattered wall. There is almost no one on the street.

The notion of asking someone – whom? – for a lift to Tibet seems absurd now that I am actually here. It is the first of August. I must be in Delhi by the end of the month, not only because of what I have written to my parents, but also because my travel pass and residence permit will have expired by that time. I retreat into calculation in order to take my mind off more immediate practicalities. I have just over four weeks – say, a week to get a lift, a week to get to Lhasa, a fortnight in Lhasa, and a couple of days to get to Kathmandu by road. There are daily flights from Kathmandu to Delhi; I should be with my family in thirty days. It is only a question, as my father is fond of telling me, of Planning Things Right.

I am disturbed from these thoughts by a few fat drops of rain that plop and sizz on the road in front of me. The desert sky is abruptly dark, and a huge gust of wind sweeps the dust off the street into a swivelling and blinding haze. A great thunderclap follows, and the rain pours down. When the haze settles I see that the cobblers and tailors have vanished. The camels, still stationed outside the bank, are staring placidly ahead. The rain is now pelting down so I look around for suitable shelter. At the next burst of thunder, I run for the first open door. I am wet through. Welcome back to the desert, I tell myself.

I am in a clothing store. The two customers pause in their buying. The shop attendants pause in their selling. The kindly old manager asks me if I am a foreigner.

'Yes,' I mumble, wringing out my new cap. I am unable to face the open-mouthed gapes of the two customers, who look like twin robots.

'You shouldn't be out in the rain, you know,' the manager gently admonishes me. 'You could catch cold.'

'You're right,' I admit, cautiously raising my eyes and immediately lowering them again; they are still gawking at me. They take in my small orange backpack, burn holes in my shoes. People often stare at you unselfconsciously in China, but this is a special performance.

'If I were you,' suggests the manager, 'I'd go and change into dry clothes the moment the rain stops.'

'Good idea.' I am about to run out of the shop, rain or no rain, when a series of electronic beeps freezes the scene into a tableau of universal amazement. It is my watch-alarm, announcing six o'clock. I press the button quickly.

The jaws of the two customers drop even further and their eyes start. I can bear it no longer. 'Why are you staring at me?' I ask. 'It makes me embarrassed.'

The first starer says, 'Don't worry, we're not looking,' and continues to stare. The second starer asks, 'How much does that watch cost? A hundred yuan? Two?'

'Leave him alone,' says the manager, rather sharply. With a slowness that would suggest that air is viscous, the twin heads turn back to their purchases. The rain stops, they leave; I decide to wait a minute or two before following them out.

But the first starer is loitering with intent. When I step outside, he accosts and grills me; and then proceeds to give me sound and detailed advice on what I should do next. It is my turn to stand open-mouthed as he sketches out a plan of action.

'Where do you want to go? Tibet? Well, that should be no problem. There's plenty of traffic going in that direction. But wait a minute. Most trucks won't be going as far as that. How about Qinghai -- say, Germu? No? Why not? You can get another lift once you're there. Yes, that's true; it's better to get a single lift at the beginning than to trust your luck in the middle of nowhere. Your best bet is to ask a few drivers where they're going. You'll find them hanging around the Tibet Transport Yard just down the road. That's where many of the trucks start from. It's almost at the end of town on the right hand side; you can't miss it. Oh yes, I forgot – you can tell a Tibetan truck in advance from the number painted on its side. If it begins with "23", it's from a work-unit in Tibet. Good luck.'

I blurt out my thanks; I do not know what to make of this bifurcated personality, this unexpected explosion of intelligence and helpfulness. I walk down the road, and there, on my right, is the sign, and inside the gate a large walled compound containing a few low buildings, a basket-ball court, and about fifty trucks, of various kinds, belonging to different work-units. Some of these units are administrative, some military. The vehicles are mainly goods trucks or else oil tankers; a few of them bear the mystic number '23'.

Three drivers are sitting on spare tyres in front of some dilapidated army trucks. They are Tibetan, and are talking animatedly about repairs, or at least so I assume, because from time to time one of them gets up with a spanner and jabs at the exposed innards of the closest vehicle. I approach them warily, not wishing to unsettle them by too sudden an appearance. When they notice my orange backpack, they turn to face me, puzzled.

'Hello,' I venture, in Chinese.

There is a pause. Then one of them, a burly man with suspicious eyes, asks me, 'Whom do you want?'

'Well, no one in particular. I came to see if I could get a lift to Tibet.'

'Your clothes are wet.'

'Yes. I got caught in the rain.'

He turns to the other two and says something in Tibetan. They look at me dubiously.

'The road is very bad,' the man continues.

'Yes, I know.'

'You don't know. The river is high at Dunhuang. The traffic is stuck there.'

'When did this happen?' I ask.

'A few days ago. The ford just south of Dunhuang is where the trouble is. The river's high and the trucks can't get through.'

The heavy rain I saw from the train must have fallen over a wider area than I had imagined. 'How far is Dunhuang?' I ask; I have been to Dunhuang once before, but feel it is best to keep talking.

'150 kilometres; you know, you'd better go to Xian or Chengdu and get a flight to Lhasa.'

'I don't have the money for that.'

'Really?' says he, his eyes on my watch.

'I suppose this truck isn't going to Lhasa, then.'

'That's right. Not until the road beyond Dunhuang is clear.'

'And then . . .?'

'The truck is under repairs,' says the man finally, with a beady look at me. 'I don't know when we will leave for Lhasa. A plane, that's the best thing.'

I get the impression that I have been dismissed. I thank him and walk towards a truck on the far side of the compound. Three more drivers are squatting on the ground nearby.

'No, there's no place in my truck,' says one, offering me a cigarette. 'But Old Wang here doesn't have any passengers.'

Old Wang appraises me as I light my cigarette. 'You said you wanted to go to Lhasa?'

'Yes.'

'There's a place in my truck. Only problem is, it's a Liberation truck, not diesel.'

'What's the difference?'

'There's no heating in a Liberation truck, and it's really cold on the way.'

'I don't mind.'

'It would be bad if you fell ill. I should get permission from my unit-leaders,' continues Old Wang in a friendly kind of way. 'Your cigarette's gone out.'

'And your unit-leaders? Which building are they in?' I ask excitedly. 'I'll speak to them if you like.'

'Oh, they're in Lhasa,' says Old Wang sadly.

A few minutes later I am standing by an oil tanker. But helpful as the driver is, he is only going as far as Germu. 'You should ask Ji over there. He goes to Lhasa regularly.'

Ji is a mild-looking old man sitting on a tyre staring at the cloudy sky. He looks benevolent, I decide, the kind of man who might be good to dumb foreigners. As I approach, he turns and asks me what I want.

I decide not to beat about the bush. 'A lift to Lhasa,' I say.

'Yesterday,' says the man.

'What? I am sorry, I don't . . .'

'Yesterday,' repeats the man, more vehemently.

'I mean . . .'

'Don't you understand Chinese?'

'I understand. It's just I thought, perhaps tomorrow . . .'

'Yesterday,' reiterates the old man. 'Our truck left yesterday for

45

Lhasa.' He looks at me with mounting annoyance. 'Why didn't you come yesterday?'

'And this truck, when will it leave?' I ask, though I am doubtful that I would want such an irascible companion.

'Where were you yesterday? You're always too late. Why didn't you come?' he demands testily.

'In Lanzhou. I didn't know about your truck,' I reply. 'Thank you for your help. Goodbye.' What he meant by my always being too late I cannot imagine. But it is, I reflect, quite true.

There are no more drivers around for me to harass. Perhaps I have been too optimistic in giving myself a week to find a lift. It could take me a month, by all indications. The Qinghai Transport Yard will certainly not have any trucks going to Tibet, so there's no point in trying there. I am hungry and tired; I should return to the hotel and come back here tomorrow. For the first time I begin to doubt whether I should have come back to Liuyuan at all, merely on the basis of the 'Lhasa' stamp in my travel pass. To make things worse, it begins to rain again.

The overcast sky merges with evening; it is soon dark. I lie on my bed eating raisins and biscuits. The silence of the night is shattered hourly by the long cries of passing trains. The desert amplifies each mournful sound and entwines it with the weak threads of my own thought. I enjoy solitude, but tonight my aloneness oppresses me like the magnified sound of blood beating in my ears. I fall asleep only towards dawn.

> Across the treeless street
> A moist breeze blows.
> I re-arrange my sheet,
> Wiggle my cold toes,
> Stare at the sky, and toss,
> Insomniac. A train
> Screams through wide plains across
> The scent of desert rain.

Liuyuan

I am too tired tonight
To sleep. I lie
Companionless. The white
Clouds gut the sky.
Orion, Pleiads, Plough,
All signs and certainties
Are lost to vision now.
The willow trees

That name the town are gone.
The freight-trains go.
The loaded trucks move on.
This is the great depot
Where nothing stays.
The hours move towards light.
Sleep: in the tall-skied days
You will forget tonight.

The next morning, by coincidence, I meet two American friends who are also students at Nanjing University. They have just returned from the Mogao grottoes at Dunhuang, a few hours to the south. They feel, like me, that the caves are beautiful but the guides worse than mediocre. An occasional corner is lit up by a torch, wielded with oppressive boredom by the woman who gives us a cursory tour around, locking up each cave as she leaves. The life of Buddha, depicted in a series of murals in one cave, is interpreted in terms of class struggle. It is more rewarding to look at pictures of the murals in a book. Nothing, however, can undermine the physical beauty of the oasis there: perfect dunes rise above a sheer wall of rock, and a salty spring feeds a few apple and apricot groves below. When I was there last month, I finally gave up listening to the guide and wandered around the orchards. Standing on a friend's shoulders I later managed to climb into a walled-up cave which the guide had ignored. It contained Tantric murals of a powerful and somewhat gymnastic sexuality.

The vast, sculpted Buddhas at Dunhuang, too large to be convenient- ly locked away from view, gaze with majesty across the oasis into the desert beyond. The influence of national variations on artistic style and of artistic style on emotional effect could not be more powerfully illustrated than by comparing images of the Buddha from different countries – the two large ones at Dunhuang, those in the Datong caves, not to mention the largest Buddha in the world, at Leshan in Sichuan, hold for me an intimidating sense of power. In the Indian Buddhas, I see by contrast a meditative calm; and in the great bronze Buddha of Kamakura in Japan, leaning slightly forward towards the people below, there is a look of compassion and tenderness so profound that its size is no longer overbearing.

In the afternoon I visit the Transport Yard again. It is sunny and clear. A few people are playing basketball in a corner, and when I walk over they ask me to join in. It turns out that they are *lingdao*, i.e. leaders or officials of various units. Two of them introduce themselves after the game. Quzha, a tall broadfaced man with a forthright manner, is Tibetan. Lin, taciturn and friendly, the older of the two, is Han. I introduce myself by my Chinese name.

'Oh,' says Quzha, 'you have a Chinese name. But you look like a foreigner to me. Where are you from?'

'Where do you think I'm from?'

'Mexico,' suggests Lin.

'No. An Asian country. Try again.'

'Sri Lanka.'

'Pakistan.'

'Nepal.'

'Iran.'

'You're getting further. It's a neighbour of China's. In fact its largest neighbour.'

'Russia?' asks Lin, bewildered. 'Surely not.'

'No, I meant . . .'

'India,' completes Quzha. 'Really?' he asks.

I nod.

48

'And what are you doing here? You're a student I expect.'

'Yes. I'm on my way home for the summer holidays.'

'Well, it's August. You won't have much time to spend at home by the time you get there.'

'Oh, I'll extend my summer holidays to midwinter if necessary,' I reply.

Quzha laughs. 'And how will you get there? Via Lhasa?'

'Yes. But it's not easy getting a lift.' I look around the yard. 'I was here yesterday but I didn't have any luck.'

'Hmm. There may be a truck or two going southward in a few days. You'd prefer a direct lift to Lhasa, I suppose?'

'Yes,' I say, though I am on the verge of lowering my sights to a truck going as far as Germu.

'Well, I'll see what I can fix up.' He smiles. 'Drop by after dinner. We're staying in that building.'

The sunset tonight in this vapid flat-roofed town is beautiful – tufts of pink and bands of yellow at the close, and the freshness of skies washed by rain. After dinner at a roadside eatery I walk down to meet Quzha again. He is about to visit a friend of his who comes from the same village in Tibet and has been working in Liuyuan for a few months. Quzha tells me to hop onto the back of his bike, and we wobble along to a bleak little room in the centre of town. I can't discover what his friend does. Quzha himself works in the Procuratorial Office of the Public Security Bureau: a position of considerable power. At the moment he is doing some work in Liuyuan, but prefers not to discuss what this work consists of.

Over glasses of foul tea, they examine my papers and the photograph of my family. ('You have grown thinner since you came to China.') I feel I'm among friends. We compare the past with the present in Tibet. Quzha's friend opens with the first words of the catechism: 'After the Gang of Four was smashed . . .', but goes on to give concrete evidence of improvements – less ideology, more religious freedom, a larger number of Tibetan cadres than before, and less witch-hunting of the politically suspect.

Quzha tells us that he was a border soldier during the Sino–Indian conflict. 'A strange task. You couldn't tell where the border was. One day it was here, another day there. We retreated, they occupied, and *vice versa*. We just did what we were told. I'm glad things have improved in our relations.'

Tonight I sleep at peace, if fitfully. Smoking, the wind and soot of the train, the dust and sand of Liuyuan, drinking tea out of other peoples' mugs and talking too much, have culminated in a sore throat and intermittent cough. As I wrap the quilt around, I remind myself that I should buy some warmer clothes.

Each time I go over to Quzha's the next day, it is with a little flare of hope. So far nothing has turned up but he is confident that it will. I, for my part, am too conscious of his kindness to ask him if there is anything in the works. He mentions that he has made enquiries. The real problem is the flooded ford at Dunhuang. Few trucks are leaving. Those that are, are full. I should remain hopeful and – this is now a constant refrain – buy some warm clothing.

I am hesitant about buying anything for the moment. I have spoken to a few more drivers about a lift but with no success. Late in the evening I visit Quzha again. I do not mention Lhasa or a ride. Finally, Quzha himself broaches the subject. 'What do you think of your chances of getting to Tibet?' he asks.

'Good,' I reply.

There may have been some scepticism in my voice, for Quzha smiles. 'How long are you prepared to wait?'

A week, I think. 'As long as necessary,' I say.

'Well, I've just arranged a ride for you in a truck going to Lhasa,' says Quzha, watching my expression with a broad smile. 'It's leaving tomorrow.'

The truck stands by the entrance to the yard. There are three people in the driving compartment, but they may be able to squeeze me in, since the driver's nephew and I are both small. Quzha introduces me to the driver Sui, about thirty-five, an alert-faced and vigorous chain-smoker, compact in limb and confident in manner. He has a permanent job with the state-owned transport unit in Lhasa to which his truck belongs. Sui is accompanied by his sulky nephew, the fifteen-year-old Xiao San ('Little Third', because he is the third son in the family). The other passenger, Gyanseng, is Tibetan. He is tall and thin, about twenty-five, and has a permanently absent-minded smile pasted onto his face. Though he speaks Chinese very well when he wishes to, he is a man of very few words.

The cargo of thermal insulating material which has just been transferred from train to truck, is for Gyanseng's unit in Lhasa. Sui is too occupied with preparations to do more than shake hands and issue a curt warning to me about the rigours ahead. The three of them are busy buying all kinds of produce that will not be available in bulk further south: watermelons, bags of watermelon seeds, and vegetables. Prices in Tibet for such things are several times the prices here. These goods are loaded on top of the cargo of insulating material, together with a spare tyre or two and a chicken-coop containing six hungry and noisy chickens. The whole thing is covered with a tarpaulin fastened by ropes. It is a diesel truck – Japanese, Isuzu – and looks sturdy and compact. Painted in white across its light blue side is the number beginning with '23'. Half the engine is uncovered, as with most trucks plying the Liuyuan–Lhasa route: this is so that the engine remains cool despite the mountainous terrain, and also so that one can examine it more quickly if a problem arises.

'You do know what you're doing, I suppose?' asks Sui. 'The road is terrible, unmetalled for half its length. And there is just one road southwards from here. If it is interrupted by flood or a landslide you can't re-route yourself: you sit and wait and get frustrated. What's more, after Germu, once you're on the plateau, it gets really cold. Of course in winter it's worse: there's the risk of freezing to death if you have to stop. But the road is dry and firm then, not the mess it is now. It's only 1,800 kilometres, but it could take us as much as ten days.'

'Oh,' I say jubilantly, 'I don't care. I won't get frustrated. I'll read – I've got a good supply of books. As for the cold, I'll buy a few warm clothes, and it'll be all right.'

'I just thought I'd warn you,' says Sui.

He drives off with Xiao San and Gyanseng to make some more

purchases, and I decide to make some of my own: biscuits, apples, peanuts, chocolate ('Lucky' brand, whose flavour I have grown used to in the past year); two packets of raisins from Turfan still remain.

I go to buy clothes at the local clothing store where I had earlier taken refuge from the rain. The shopgirl asks me what I want.

'I'd like to buy a padded jacket.'

'No padded jackets.' She turns away.

'Are there padded trousers?'

She turns back, wearily. 'No padded trousers.'

'But I've seen people on the street wearing them. There aren't any other clothing stores in town.'

'Come back in winter.'

'Isn't there anything made of thick material, anything warm at all?'

'No. Come back in winter.' She yawns.

'Please listen. My problem is that I'm leaving for Lhasa today . . .'

'Yes, try Lhasa.'

'. . . and anything that could protect me from the cold would be useful. Do you have any warm underwear in stock?'

'No.'

'Even a tracksuit would help.'

She stares at me. 'You want to wear a tracksuit to Lhasa?'

'Yes.'

She pulls a blue tracksuit out from a shelf and plumps it down on the counter with a dismissive air. I am glad that it is my size so I won't have to make any further requests. I read the price tag and take out my wallet.

'I'll buy it. Oh, and a pair of those socks, too.'

She clicks the abacus, and says as she does so, 'You need cotton coupons for the tracksuit.'

'I don't have any.'

The fingers stop in mid-calculation. 'Well, you can't buy it then.'

'What? But . . . look . . . please, this is very important.'

'You must have cotton coupons.'

'If I don't have something warm to wear I'll freeze to death.'

'It's the regulation.'

'I'm leaving for Lhasa today. It's . . .'

'Yes, yes,' she says, cutting me short. 'You've said all that before. But regulations are regulations.'

I try another tactic: fight regulation with regulation. There are so many of them that no one can possibly know them all. I speak severely: 'You must know that foreigners do not require cotton coupons to make purchases.'

'Everyone needs them.'

'Ah, but I have bought a cotton jacket in the Beijing Friendship Store without coupons.' (This is true, but she is clearly unconvinced.) 'We have to use this kind of money instead.' Saying this, I take out a note of funny money. 'This is the regulation for foreigners. And what is valid in the capital of the country must be true in a small unimportant town like Liuyuan.' (RxR ch!)

'Oh.' A crack in the defence. Then an attempt at a rally: 'But our regulations are different.'

To maintain the initiative, I bring another piece into play. 'Take me to see your *lingdao*,' I say. 'Where is the manager of the shop?' I look around for the kindly man who had been here two days ago.

'He's busy. He's eating lunch.' She folds up the tracksuit to put it away. Evasive play and feeble counterattack, I decide.

'Good. Then he'll have plenty of time to listen to me without interruption.'

'No, no,' she says, conceding defeat. 'Wait here. I'll go and get him.' (BxQ; resigns.)

The manager, who was not, in fact, having lunch, listens gravely to my request, and looks closely at the funny money. 'Yes, I'll accept this,' he says finally, and to the shop assistant, 'He doesn't need coupons.' He turns back to me. 'I'm sorry you had so much trouble. It's not her fault. She was just following instructions.' He pauses. 'Is there anything else you want?'

'No. Thank you for your help.'

'No, no, don't thank me,' says the manager. 'We must take care of our foreign friends.'

Gyanseng and Xiao San pack my luggage on top, between a spare tyre and a big bag of watermelon seeds. We say goodbye to Quzha, and set out at about four in the afternoon. The truck is small, the driving cabin cramped. The cabin is full of the most varied paraphernalia: small tools, rags, boxes, packets of cigarettes, food, magazines, a spade, and a sheepskin that covers the seat, and which has a strong odour of lanolin that even the smell of petrol and cigarettes cannot mask. The windscreen, like the rest of the cabin, is none too clean. The glove compartment clatters open every few minutes and has to be slammed shut again. The horn works only too well. So, luckily, do the windscreen wipers, usually a weak feature on Chinese trucks; the rear-view mirrors, which often get broken off are, I notice, intact. The driver's section, to the left, is divided off by the gear lever. The other half fits two people, but with three of us and a couple of bags and boxes at our feet, the discomfort is acute. We change places from time to time. The seat near the window, at least during the warmer section of the journey, is the spot to have. The passenger sitting in the middle is squashed between his two fellows, while the passenger on the far left is prodded by the driver's elbow whenever he changes gear. When I hold this place, Sui's elbow is driven impartially into my guts in between amiable exchanges about the state of the road.

Liuyuan lies at the periphery of the so-called Black Gobi. Coal-black hummocks and hills rise around us as we leave the town, smoothing slowly into black plain, so flat that it is impossible to discern any rise, or to guess at our altitude – judging from any physical indications, we could be anywhere from 100 metres to 3,000 metres above sea-level. Later, the black gives way to reds and pinks, soft cupped and conical mounds rising up from the desert. The little scrub there has been thins out even further. Herds of Bactrian camel appear, shaking their lopsided humps and chewing the thorny vegetation as they watch the trucks and camel-carts go by. We are travelling very fast along a bumpy stretch of road; a couple of watermelons fall off the top of the truck. In little over an hour, the sandy soil sprouts tufts of green, patches of bush and reed, a tree or two. A hawk with upturned wingtips flies past. There must be an oasis nearby. We turn off the main road to visit a friend of Sui's, who lives on a farm there.

We have barely sat down when Xiao San comes running in from the truck where he has been standing guard.

'How many pieces of luggage did you have?' he asks me.

'Two,' I reply.

'Oh, good,' says Xiao San, looking at the small black bag I have with me. 'I was worried. One of the ropes has got loose and some more watermelons have fallen off. But your bag is still there.'

'My *bag*?! But I had two on top. I wasn't counting this one.'

'Oh no!' says Sui, jumping up. 'We'd better try to find it at once.'

We rush back along the road to Liuyuan, looking out for the large black bag that has fallen off. Books, clothing and some of my research materials are in it. At the 60 km. milestone we see some roadworkers' tents, so we stop to make enquiries.

'You haven't seen a black bag lying by the road, have you?' says Sui.

Mr Wang is a short, sturdy-looking man. 'Yes,' he says, 'but it couldn't have been yours.

I describe the bag. Mr Wang looks puzzled.

'It certainly looked like that. I saw it lying by the side of the road and picked it up. A few seconds later a truck going towards Liuyuan stopped. The driver claimed that the bag belonged to a truck from his unit, and he went off with it. He seemed to know what he was talking about.'

'How long ago was this?'

'About half an hour ago.'

'Can you describe the truck?'

'I didn't think of taking down the number at the time, but I have the impression that it was from Qinghai. It was a diesel truck, like yours. I can't remember the unit the truck came from.' Mr Wang pauses. 'Coming to think of it, I didn't notice any trucks like that one going towards Liuyuan earlier. And the bag was on the wrong side of the road, too. If I had given it any thought, I would have known his story was false. *Ta-ma-de!*' he swears under his breath. 'He really fooled me.'

'Would you recognise him if you saw him again?' asks Sui.

'Yes. He was middle-aged, had a sort of fattish face . . .'

'Look, comrade,' interrupts Sui, 'Could I trouble you to come with us to Liuyuan? He must have gone there, but unless we're quick he could make off again. And we don't have a chance of identifying him without you.'

'Sure,' says the energetic Mr Wang. We drop Xiao San off at the tents to make room in the truck. Sui tells him to wait there till we return.

Hot on the trail, but with few clues, we return to Liuyuan and head straight for the police station. On hearing from Sui that the luggage of a foreigner has been stolen, they are most perturbed. An angry swarm of officers comes buzzing out of the police station, and we go to hunt for the truck. We split into two groups, each accompanied by police officers, and scour the town: move from street to street, walled yard to walled yard, work-unit to work-unit, but all to no avail. We return disappointed; perhaps the thief has gone on already. I am asked to write down a list of objects in the lost bag: books, underwear, shirts, shorts, tracksuit, research forms, straw hat, wind-jacket, dictionary, raisins . . . in my agitation I forget the characters for 'raisin'. Suddenly Mr Wang rushes in: he and Sui have found the offending driver sitting in his truck in front of the railway station.

When Wang pointed out the truck to Sui, Sui told him to wait there, and walked over to it. The driver initially denied that there was any bag in the truck. But when Sui jumped into the cabin and found it there, lying at the driver's feet, he said, 'Oh, that bag? I just picked that up from the roadside and was going to take it to the police.' The bag was open, and the things lying in disarray inside.

The police go to bring in the driver for questioning. I sit and drink tea. We are kept in separate rooms. He is being cross-examined, and the police tell me that he is displaying a 'bad attitude'. He has also drunk a lot, and this does not improve his consistency. He can't explain why he rummaged through the things, nor why he told Wang that the bag had been dropped by a colleague of his, nor why he just told Sui that he had picked it up himself. Above all, he is bewildered by how quickly we have followed him. And indeed, if it hadn't been for Sui's stopping to meet a friend, or Xiao San checking the ropes, or Sui reacting to the loss with such speed and initiative, or Wang going out of his way to help us, or the prompt police assistance, we would not have recovered the bag. Indeed we might even now be blithely and blindly bumping along towards Dunhuang.

I am brought into the room where the driver is sitting on a bench. He looks a little forlorn; I turn to the bag. As I touch it, he glares at me.

'You should take better care of your things.'

I don't reply, and he continues aggressively.

'I brought your things back. If it hadn't been for me you would have lost them.'

This last remark draws blood. 'I know what happened,' I retort heatedly, 'and what I'd like to know, is why you opened the bag and turned things upside down if you only wanted to . . .'

'Please, Mr Xie,' says a policeman to me. 'Calm down. We'll do the questioning if you don't mind. If you could just check that nothing is missing . . .' As each item comes out, it is put on a list: Mr Long calls them out, and Mr Duan writes them down. Nothing is missing.

It is night, and raining. We drop in to see Quzha for a few minutes before setting off again. He is amazed to see us. Sui is not pleased to see Xiao San, who has hitched a lift back to Liuyuan, and scolds him roundly for leaving the roadworkers' tents. There are now five of us in the truck. We beg some petrol off one of Sui's petrol-station acquaintances, though it is after hours – 'special circumstances', pleads Sui – and drive back towards Dunhuang, half asleep. The headlights of oncoming trucks look unbearably bright, miles before we pass them. When we arrive at the roadworkers' tents, I try to give Wang two packets of Kent. He refuses at first, embarrassed that I should have offered him something for what he'd done more than willingly, but I tell him how bad I'll feel if I can't make even a trivial gesture in return.

At 1.30 in the morning we roll into Dunhuang: the town is dead and the Transport Yard full. It takes all of Sui's eloquence on the subject of 'special circumstances' to get us a bed for the night.

5

Dunhuang:

of floods and feasts

Sui and Gyanseng look at the floodwaters, and then, somewhat regretfully, at me.

'Well,' says Sui, 'I don't think we'll be able to go through today, either. But look, whatever happens, I'm sure the river will subside tomorrow. The road has been cut off for a week now, and it hasn't rained in the last two days. If it hadn't been for the reservoir up there, the water would have stopped by now.' The Dang River Reservoir, which supplies the desert fields, is overfull because of the recent heavy rains, and water is being released to ease the pressure on its dam. Through every one of the channels that runs towards the corn, wheat and vegetable fields at Dunhuang and finally disperses into the desert, the floodwaters swirl and churn, swift and yellow-brown with sand and silt. It is awesome to watch; all around are dunes and plains of sand, whilst in the middle the water rushes past the fields, superfluous and irrelevant. But here, just beyond the town, where the road leads south towards Qinghai and Tibet, the waters are untrammelled by any man-made walls. They scour the bed of the River Dang, plunge on past the southern margin of the town, through the ruins of the bridge destroyed two years ago by flood, around the concrete pillars of the new bridge under construction, and across the ford, which is our one means of continuing southwards. Trucks are lined up on the approaches to the ford on both sides of the flooded river, and a few intrepid drivers are attempting to plunge their way through.

Xiao San has disappeared. I look around for him, and spot him eventually, laughing with a bunch of kids a few yards away, up by the uncompleted approaches to the new bridge. Half the juvenile and much of the adult population of Dunhuang have gathered at the site to survey the proceedings, and are assessing the chances of the few trucks that attempt to cross the river. Xiao San is expounding to his group – 'That's a Liberation Truck – it uses petrol, and if anything happens to its ignition, it's finished – I bet it doesn't make it across.' True to prediction, the truck, after butting its way bravely through the spate, suddenly splutters and stalls. A diesel truck, despite its low-slung chassis, makes it across, tilting first this way and then that, but without mishap. A third, this time an oil tanker, manoeuvres carefully along the ford (invisible under the swollen waters), then suddenly slips off into the sandy bed, and, to our horror, begins to sink until only the top of its cabin is left above the brown surface of the river. The driver manages to clamber out. From now on, the unfortunate vehicle acts both as a marker of the margins of the ford, and as an example of the perils of relaxed vigilance. Nevertheless, by mid-morning, the river is littered with trucks, wallowing like hippopotami in various stages of submersion; and yet more trucks try to make it through. The crowd enjoys this. When a truck gets stuck, they cheer. When a truck gets through, they cheer.

This is our second day in Dunhuang. As we walk back to our truck, Sui makes a few soothing remarks. It's not worth the risk today, he says; we'll definitely try to leave tomorrow. Meanwhile we can buy some more fruit and vegetables to take with us to Lhasa. He wanders off to the free market nearby to haggle over grapes and eggplants. I sit by the truck, fend off the flies, and open a book by Naipaul that my American friends have left me – *India: A Wounded Civilization*. Behind me three drivers are shouting about the price of tomatoes.

Now the chickens on top of the truck are cackling. One of them has laid an egg. Sui tries to get the egg out of the cage, and is soundly pecked. He then bribes the chicken with watermelon peel, after which the pecking becomes more sporadic. He inveigles the egg out, and I put it in the plastic bag with the grapes. We then continue to load the truck with the baskets of vegetables and fruit that he has just bought. Xiao San and Gyanseng stand below and pass them up to Sui and me. Watermelons at eight cents a *jin*, and very sweet: 'You have to know how to bargain,' says Sui modestly.

Sui has a friend who lives on a commune not far from the dunes. It is an old house of mud and brick, with a courtyard, trellises of grapes, and ancient trees: pear and apple and apricot. The apricots of Dunhuang are marvellous, but just now they are past their prime, while the pears, though sweetish, are not quite ripe. In a sty near the house a couple of pigs grunt friendlily as unripe and overripe vegetables are thrown over to them. The large private plot supplies most of our dinner: gourds and melons, eggplants and tomatoes (tomato, in Chinese, is a 'barbarian eggplant'), *baocai* and *jiucai* and capsicum and chillies.

A private plot is the land allotted by the commune to a family for its own personal use. Below 10 per cent of arable land is usually thus distributed among commune members. A few vegetables from the private plot, a pig or chickens reared by the family, perhaps some piecework or local handicraft: these supplement the family's income from working on the commune fields. Because of the time and effort expended on private plots, their productivity exceeds that of the commune fields. (This is also true, and to a far greater extent, of the Soviet Union.) Certain recent rural reforms in effect divide even the commune fields out among families, setting state quotas for production. Since anything in excess of this is kept by the family, it is hoped that the incentives created will lead to increased production.

After the main course, we have noodles, and bread flavoured with spices. Sui complains that there is no meat. 'You know how it is,' says our host. 'At the Spring Festival we slaughter a lamb, say, and then there is plenty of meat for a while. But kill a pig or a lamb now, in midsummer, and it'll rot.' People here, in Dunhuang, whether Han or Muslim, eat a fair amount of mutton; in the eastern provinces it is not much liked, owing to its strong odour. People all over China eat pork (except for Muslims) and beef and fish if they are available, and chicken and duck; but dog, which I have enjoyed twice in Nanjing, is not eaten here in the western provinces. Dog meat is red, eaten in winter for its 'warming' properties, and tastes excellent roasted with red chillies.

My host turns to me and asks me why foreigners eat so many tomatoes. He takes 80 *jin* of tomatoes every day to the hotel where foreigners stay, and 60 *jin* a day to the guest house. I am baffled. The price change, as he describes it, is interesting: from 45 cents per *jin* in the off-season, to 30 cents, to the present 15 cents. I remember being surprised in Nanjing once, when the price fell to five cents; but then vegetable produce (with the exception of Chinese cabbage, which can be stored) is highly perishable. The price as a result is very dependent on the state of the local supply.

After dinner I watch the coffee-coloured floodwaters swirling past in a canal. Sheep bleat in a distant field, and bicycles overtake a donkey-cart on the country road. The flies disappear. A line of very tall, slim poplars sways against the sky. I follow the canal, then a road, and finally a dirt track down to the boundary between the sand and the sown. In a field of corn surrounded by a deep green hedge of marijuana plants, I see a mud building that looks like a Buddhist temple. I cross the field, and see that it is in ruins. Goats graze amongst the rubble. Weeds and a few sunflowers have overgrown it, and its rooms and cells are open to the sky. Stubs of broken beams protrude from the scorched walls. Someone has written a poem in Chinese in white chalk on these blackened walls:

'This day Zhi Xiong came to the old temple.
He came from far away with no other intention
Than to see the ancient temple,
And he saw it and wept.'

I stand in that lonely place for a while, and feel like weeping myself. A line from Leopardi comes to mind – 'And now above the cities the goat browses.' But for him it was Vesuvius that destroyed and nullified the works of man, while here the burnt walls speak of a sadder, more purposeful, more purposeless destruction. The marijuana hedges are in flower; there is a curious intoxication in the evening air. An old man whom I question on the road tells me the temple was pulled down and burnt in the Cultural Revolution, the monks beaten to death or driven away. 'It was mainly young people from Dunhuang town, and a few Red Guards,' he explains. 'No one has ever dared to build it up again.'

It is almost sunset. He gives me a lift on his donkey-cart, and we trot along, not exchanging further words. He offers me a cigarette; I accept. A little further on, I get off, and start walking towards the dunes, deep golden in this light, and very large. The small white thorn bushes throw shadows several times their height onto the slightly rippled sand. I climb the ridge of the largest dune, one from which I hope to see the sun set over the whole oasis of Dunhuang. It is steep, and I pause several times to take a drink from my waterbottle. I reach the top a few minutes before sunset. The sand is still very warm.

Far below me to the left are a few squares of harvest-ripe yellow wheat and a crescent-shaped pool, and to the far right the dunes stretch out towards the Buddhist grottoes. In front, the world lies flat, green and gold, the poplars and corn ending abruptly in the distance, where the sand resumes. The gorged waters of the Dang River look thin and innocuous from this distance. The electric lights come on over Dunhuang, and shimmer through the levels of cooling air. It is quite still.

I look down towards the ruins of the temple. From here, this tall mound of sand, it is possible to be detached from human effort and human frenzy. Above, the sky, marked with a few residual clouds, changes to a deep red, and the sun sinks over the vague horizon of the desert. For a few minutes afterwards, the underside of the clouds reflects a sun already invisible, and by a strange tilt of light the sky actually appears to become brighter. Then the angle changes, the clouds turn grey, and above me is a sky of deep indigo. In this desert night the Milky Way is brilliantly clear. It strikes me how descriptive of its meandering course is its Chinese name, the Silver River.

Sui coughs and smokes and coughs. At night he reads, then pauses to cough, then spits on the floor. The sputum is green and viscous; I am quite worried about him. I make a few indirect references to the perils of smoking; Sui looks up momentarily from his short story to agree with me, then returns to his reading. When the cigarette has burned down to a stub, he holds it in his yellowed fingers and lights the next one, coughs and carries on. When he smokes, he has no special expression of pleasure on his face, any more than most people have when merely breathing.

'Lao Sui,' I say in the Chinese form of address to a (usually elder) friend, 'This smoking of yours, have you ever tried to give it up?'

Sui grunts; he realises I am not going to let him enjoy his story or his cigarettes, so he turns his magazine upside down on the pillow, open at his page. 'Yes – sometimes I do. Everyone tells me to. I'm sure I can if I want to.'

'Well then . . .'

'But I don't want to. There's nothing to do on the road except smoke. There's no radio, I am not that taken by the scenery – I've been doing this route for years. It gets boring.'

'But you've been smoking for years. Doesn't that get boring too?'

Sui laughs. It turns into a cough. 'No. It helps me to concentrate.' He pauses to think for a while. 'And the few times I've given it up have been when I've miscalculated the length of the journey – you know, if there have been unexpected floods or landslides – and I've run out. But I get pretty irritable when that happens.'

I decide that these are the classic responses of a stubborn smoker, and that he may respond to some classic nagging. So over the next few days, I manage, by dint of some cheerful prodding, to get him down to a little under a pack a day. But, while this doesn't sour relations – Sui is, after a fashion, keen to cure his cough and therefore tolerant of my interference – it makes me feel uncomfortable, and eventually I give up an already faltering effort.

I wake up in the morning to the buzz of flies. It has rained during the night, and the yard is a field of mud, trucks on its edge and the boiler-room in the middle. The boiler-room is the one source of hot water; I take a wash-basin (with a 'Double Happiness' marriage symbol on it) and manoeuvre myself across the yard on islands of solid earth. With a scrubbed face and brushed teeth, I feel able to face things again.

It is wet and miserable beyond belief, water pouring in fat ropes from a yellow-grey sky onto the brown paste of the ground. It is obvious that we won't be able to leave today. It is hard to remember that we are in the desert.

I wonder when Sui will get up. His hours are curious. He can work and read (smoking continuously) until three in the morning or later, suddenly collapsing to wake up after noon. Xiao San, who has been made to sleep in the truck in order to guard it, is aggrieved with his uncle. 'Wake him up! Wake him up!' he says when I go over to the truck to see how he is. 'Why are we just sitting here? Other trucks have left across the ford. We should have gone yesterday. Now we're stuck here – it could be weeks. I'll never get to Germu at this rate. It's eleven o'clock – why don't you wake him up?'

I compromise with Xiao San, and wake Sui up at noon. He looks surprised, then agitated when he notices what time it is; we walk quickly over to the truck, and he starts up the engine. But then his eye falls on one of Xiao San's comic books, a detective story, and he begins turning over the pages. It is twenty minutes before he looks up. 'Oh, I forgot,' he says, and drives the engine out onto the street in the direction of the free market.

The free market is the natural complement to the private plots and handicrafts that supplement a peasant's income. Certain items are sold only at the price fixed by the government, others may have a fixed price ceiling, and yet others may be sold at any price that demand establishes.

In the state markets, prices are, by and large, rigid; until certain recent reforms were introduced, there was no incentive for those who ran them to respond in a flexible way to increases in demand. Free markets, on the other hand, provide incentive in its most naked form to those who produce with sale in mind. During the ideologically inflexible years of the Cultural Revolution, such markets were banned, and private plots (the source of most of the produce) also came under attack. But now that restrictions have been lifted, both private plots and markets are flourishing. Produce at the private markets is usually fresh, and some things (e.g. fish or eggs) are often available here when they are not elsewhere. The men and women selling their wares, who come up from the countryside specifically for this purpose, show an enthusiasm for clinching a sale that contrasts powerfully with the lackadaisical indifference of their counterparts in state markets.

The free market at Dunhuang is a sight to behold. Donkeys haul in the produce, old men and women then sell it. For all the bustle and colour, there is not too much shouting or calling out of wares. One man is sleeping beside his bag of seeds; he twitches when flies settle on his hands. A child bursts into tears and is pacified by being given a piece of dried apricot. Flies settle on it instantly. (The flies of Dunhuang are monstrous and innumerable.) Tomatoes, eggplants, capsicums, melons, rat poison, fox furs, sugar, sweets, herbs, insoles for shoes, combs, spices – the free market has all of these. There are small disparities in price from stall to stall, so I try my hand at bargaining.

It is now our third day at Dunhuang and the floods are still too high to risk the ford. We have all seen the caves before, so we kill time by walking around the streets. There is a good Muslim restaurant on the main street, where you can get roasted chunks of lamb dipped in hot sauce. There is an ice-cream parlour where a rich, creamy-yellow ice-cream is made from fresher ingredients than I have tasted anywhere else in China. Sui buys some trinkets and artificial flowers for friends whom he will see on the way to Lhasa, and a yet more elaborate plastic flower arrangement for his wife. Later we go out to a commune to buy some corn, which I am sent to get ground.

At twilight, I sit on a log by the truck; Sui joins me and we share a watermelon. He has just returned from doing a few errands for friends, and is now tired and sweaty. Sui rarely refuses people who ask him for help; yet his kindness is tempered by an intelligence that quickly tells him if he is being used. With his friends he is not over-polite – as when he complained yesterday about there not being any meat – but if his manner is abrupt, it is only that he expects the same straightforwardness from others.

Sui eats chunk after chunk of watermelon. 'I may as well eat as many as I can now,' he remarks. 'They won't be anything like as good by the time we get to Lhasa.' He talks about home. With a job like his, he's on the road most of the time. He gets ten days of rest in Lhasa after a round trip to Liuyuan, and then sets out again. He especially misses his wife. 'You must miss your family, too,' he says.

'Yes, more and more lately; as I grow older it has an anomalous effect on me. Independence doesn't seem to have anything to do with it. But I shall be home within the month.'

'I hope so,' says Sui. 'But someone told me yesterday that the road ninety kilometres south of Dunhuang has also been cut off by floods and is not passable. It might take a long time to get to Germu.'

'And after Germu?'

'Oh, it gets worse. Then we're on the Qinghai–Tibet plateau. Mud and mountains. And altitude sickness – it doesn't affect me but it will probably trouble you. The journey to Germu is bliss compared to what comes after.'

I chop off another chunk of watermelon and we eat in silence for a while.

'Well, at least it'll be more comfortable in the truck after Germu,' I venture. 'Xiao San's getting off at his parents'.'

'Yes, there's that. And I think Gyanseng has had enough truck travel, too – he'll try to get a plane ticket to Lhasa. The problem is that there are only two planes a week, and everyone wants to fly, as there are floods all over western China and the land routes are difficult. He'll be lucky if he manages to get one.'

'Is something the matter with Gyanseng?' I ask. 'He doesn't look too well and hardly says a word. He's even stopped smiling.'

'I don't think so,' says Sui. 'It's just that he's tired, and bored, and misses Lhasa. Also, he knows what the road's like after Germu; he came down from Lhasa to Liuyuan with me in the truck this time. But then Gyanseng doesn't talk too much – as you've noticed – so it's difficult to know for sure. I'm more worried about Xiao San. He's not a bad kid, but he's been sullen and rude recently. At first, he enjoyed escaping from his parents, but he's homesick after a month of it, and wants to get back to Germu as soon as possible.'

'All four of us seem to be homesick.' We laugh.

'Well, yes, let's hope the water doesn't rise again tomorrow. Then we can go to Nanhu.'

'What's that?'

'A small oasis a couple of hours south of here. We'll spend the night there; there are some things I need to do. Xiao San won't be pleased; if he were behind the wheel we wouldn't stop until we got to my sister's door.' Sui flips some watermelon peel into the night.

'Buy him a few comic books,' I suggest. 'He seems to enjoy them.'

Sui smiles at me. 'I'm sorry about this morning,' he says. 'I just didn't notice what I was doing. When I start reading, I lose all sense of time. Good books, good movies, good cigarettes are my obsessions. Comics aren't good reading, I suppose, but once I begin one, I've just got to finish it.'

6

Nanhu:

an oasis interlude

The next day dawns crisp and clear, and the floodwaters have fallen a little. Sui surveys the situation and decides we should cross today. The oil tanker is still lying in mid-river, but most of the other trucks have been hauled out by tractor. Suddenly Sui remembers that he has promised a friend in Lhasa that he will visit his parents in Dunhuang. We turn back towards the town. The caretaker, his wife and granddaughter live in a rickety wooden shack by an empty building yard. The wife kills flies with expert movements of her delicate hands. The granddaughter does sums aloud. The old man tells Sui to take a cardboard crate loaded with things his son may need in Lhasa. We return to the ford.

Sui then remembers that he has to buy a few more chickens, so we return to the free market. By noon we are back at the ford. A system has now been set up for orderly crossing: men holding red and green flags signal from each shore. Previously it was difficult to prevent trucks from trying to cross simultaneously from both banks. At the moment the main problem is that a convoy of heavy trailers carrying oil exploration equipment is blocking the approaches to the ford on our side.

When the way is finally unclogged, we begin to cross. The crossing is an anticlimax. We splash and lurch a little but Sui has a steady hand and we are soon on the opposite shore. We are hastily beckoned onwards by the men with coloured flags, and we continue the short journey to Nanhu. The view to our left is remarkable: a long range of golden dunes, revealing as they become lower a razor-sharp backbone of red rock underneath. Behind them stands a range of snow-clad peaks. We are clearly still in the desert: there is a mirage to the right, an unstable watery shimmer reflecting low hills. A few tree-packed oases, discrete and pleasing to the eye, stand in the midst of the aridity around. We leave the main road, bound for one of these. Fields appear, and houses, and a deep blue lake. This is Nanhu, or 'South Lake'.

We stop the truck a short distance from the lake, and walk across hay-scented fields to the house of a friend of Sui's who is with the army, stationed at Lhasa. His wife has come back here to their old house in the village to have her child. The Lhasa air is too thin; after the child is one or two years old, she will move back. (Children are precious. You can only have two, and in the cities the recommended number is one.) The woman is shy but very hospitable. While she talks to us her child feeds at her breast, and her niece looks in at us from the doorway. The courtyard of the large brick-built peasant house is cool. Xiao San, who is outside, guarding the truck with the philosophical Gyanseng, complains of a headache, and is hot and hungry and angry. 'I hate guarding the truck. I'll never guard the truck again,' he raves at his uncle. But after a lunch of bread and chives and soya sauce he cheers up and reverts to the sulky-cheerful prankster he is. He delights in annoying his uncle, and when Sui goes off to do some work in the village, he looks around for other prey. I manage to elude him by going off for a swim in the lake, a few minutes' walk from the house.

There are actually two lakes, I discover, both fed by springs. There is a larger, broader, very clear lake below, and above it a narrower, serpentine lake of yet more amazing cleanliness, almost as pure as Heaven Lake, near Urumqi. It is paradise on a hot day like this. I sit on the sand in the shade of reeds; nearby a tree leans out over the water. I swim across and back a few times, and then just splash randomly about for an hour or two. I feel ecstatically free in the water, moving in three dimensions and bursting upwards into the warm air, and it is my first bath – not counting occasional hot water scrubs – for a week. The lake is cool, but warm bands stretch sensuously across it. A tractor occasionally pauses on the upper road, a girl comes down to the edge to fill a couple of buckets of water on a shoulder pole. A woman brings a buffalo down to the lake. Three or four naked children play in the shallows. Sui comes down after a while: 'I'd better take care of you. You're a foreigner; I don't want you drowning,' he says.

The water gurgles as it runs out of the upper lake. The air is dry. The occasional cry of a bird or the hum of a bee punctuates our talk. There are, thank God, fewer flies here. White butterflies fly past the reeds, small, deliberate, thin-legged insects crawl on the sand, cumbersome yet delicate; and swift sand ants scurry to and fro. Sui lights up a cigarette and resumes coughing. When I tell him to give it up, he tells me to sell my tape-recorder. Late in the afternoon, after a short swim, he strolls back to the house. I stay by the lake for a while.

At evening I walk along the shore of the upper lake. To the west is the sunset, and eastwards the elongated lake leads to a green valley and then scrub, and finally nothing, desert. Perfect reflections of reed and bird and cloud are poised in the clear water, a pebble from my hand or bird droppings the only things that ripple the surface. Flights of pigeons swoop down like dive-bombers in a war comic, down from the mud cliffs on one side to the ten-foot-tall reeds, down to the water surface, and then up again. Four young men wielding spades come up and exchange a friendly hello. They tell me the lake freezes over in winter; temperatures fall to −30°C. While they talk they absently knock some scrub down with their spades. They have been clearing the road ahead all day; a landslide near the Dangjin Pass had blocked the road to Qinghai, but we'll be able to go through tomorrow. Tonight there's going to be an open air movie, arranged by the commune authorities at Nanhu. Why don't I see it, they suggest, instead of wasting my time walking around? They saunter off in the direction of the village. A light breeze begins to blow. It grows dark, then quickly cold. For dinner we have lentils and noodles. I sleep on a large wooden double bed in the house; Sui's muffled snores vibrate through the still night air from across the courtyard.

Early morning. Woken up by insistent cock-crow, I go for a walk to the lake and brush my teeth by a small pond. It is a lovely morning and the lake surface is smooth, except where a breeze or a duck ruffles it. A man walking to the fields with hoe on shoulder calls out a greeting. The people here, though curious, do not stare. I sit by the lake and feel a delicious calm swing through me.

Suddenly the ear-shattering cacophony of 'exercise music' blares out.

This wretched institution, by which most of the inhabitants of China are jolted out of their thoughts or sleep and instructed by loudspeaker to bend and twist and rotate, aborts the mood of serenity that the place had created. On a visit to Chengde, the old imperial summer resort not far from Beijing, I was wandering through the grounds of the deserted temples when loudspeakers began to shriek noises identical to these from across the river. The Chinese themselves like it no better than foreigners do, but it is difficult to change things once they've begun. In the Chinese dormitory at Nanjing University, our ears were invaded every morning at six by this atrocious blast. I now see that it follows one wherever one is in the country.

As I pass through a corridor of sunflowers on the way back to the house, I encounter a dog who tries to lick me and a goat who tries to butt me. At the house, the mother is breast-feeding the insatiable baby. Her six-year-old niece looks on and laughs. From defiant curiosity and dread of me she has progressed to friendly mimickry. She is called Xiexie, and has small plaits. Together we watch three boys unload cartloads of sand by the wall outside the house. They then drive the donkey-carts on with cries of 'kirrik! kirrik!' A wall is to be built nearby, or perhaps this wall is to be strengthened: Xiexie only speaks the local dialect and I can catch perhaps one word in three of her explanation.

It is still early in the morning when we set out from Nanhu across the desert and past the oases. We climb steadily, seeing a purple snow-capped range in the distance; we enter a weak and broken stretch of road, the result of desert rains and floods, and then a valley with scrubby grass, a Kazakh hut or two, a white horse, some roadworkers clearing away the debris of the recent landslide. Xiao San is increasingly aggressive. He tells me, when I point out corn in an oasis field, that it is millet. When I say I can see a snow-peak, he says there are only dunes. I give him a couple of aspirin for his headache.

We cross the Dangjin Pass, over 4,000 metres high, by noon, and descend from the province of Gansu into the province of Qinghai. Sui is not used to waking up early, and now pulls the truck over to the side. He sleeps for an hour. The chickens cluck and the wind whistles past. Xiao San gets out and lies in the shade of the truck.

7

The Chaidam Basin

By afternoon we descend into a pastel-coloured basin, also treeless, and with wide horizons; blues of sky and lake and distant ranges, purples and browns of the soil, white clouds, every colour is light, pastel, delicate. A wind is blowing, so it's cool. In winter this place must be desolately cold. I take a few photographs: grassless, treeless, birdless stone and pebble and rock.

We cross the basin, rise gently for a while, and as we reach the point of maximum elevation, see in front of us a breathtaking sight: a vast slope, as far as the eye can see, as if the world itself sloped, a declivity that stretches for perhaps a hundred miles ahead of us; and this plain has ridges rising from its floor, but they are low, short ridges, and well-spaced, so that you can see the plain continue beyond them. The ridges are of pink and slate and purple rock, with cloud-shadows falling on some of them – and the earth to the right is beige and ochre and fawn. On the tops of the north-facing peaks there is a touch of snow. A little later, snow and cloud are joined by a different white, that of stretches of salt undissolved on this arid plain. Then comes a feast of geological transformations: nude dunes, unconnected by sand, completely isolated one from another; then black hills, oily and stony, slowly becoming wrinkled and clay-like; later, lakes of a distant blue, with a band of sparse vegetation in front, and a red strip of soil nearest us, like the uninvented tricolour of an artists' republic. A sole gold mountain glows in the late light; camels graze on a green plain; the combed raked clouds are yellowed with sunset; and finally there is darkness, and a salt lake, and the distant lights of Germu.

The road so far is fairly good, except where it is undergoing repair;

there temporary and muddy diversions cause us to jolt and slither. The first section of the road was metalled, and there is a plan to metal the entire Liuyuan-Lhasa route. (The present dirt-road has to be flattened every year after the rainy season.) From time to time we come across the People's Liberation Army engaged in road construction on a grand scale, with the help of some machinery but mainly spades. These troops work here for half the year. When the winter winds freeze the land they return to Germu or Xining or Lanzhou, making the region even more isolated than before.

For Sui, the scenery of this unpopulated terrain is only occasionally captivating, as when under some transitory slant of light an unusual gold touches the evening hills. The dunes and plains, the pale basin of the Chaidam, all the permanent features of the landscape, are fixtures along a route he has travelled every month for years. He is inured to their beauty; his pleasures along the road are mainly social: talk, food where good food can be obtained, haggling in the market, visiting friends. There is no radio in his truck, and when he isn't talking he is smoking. He looks his thirty-five years. His face is somewhat full, though he has features sharp for a Han Chinese. His black hair, unkempt despite the comb he often uses, is pushed back from his forehead whenever it obstructs his vision. His teeth, like his fingers, are nicotine-stained. His eyes are wonderfully alert and friendly, except that, when he is busy with various errands and preparations, they cloud over with an abstraction almost impossible to pierce until the job is completed.

He has an intuitive practicality. His truck has grown so much a part of him that the occasional repairs he makes are carried out almost unconsciously, as if he were scratching his arm. The truck could be rattling along with fifteen loud mechanical noises merging in counterpoint: Sui is unconcerned. A sixteenth, seemingly harmless, joins them: he is instantly alert, pulls the truck over, jumps out of the cabin and prods about the engine, unscrewing caps, checking for oil and water, plugging leaks, joining wires. When he gets back into the cabin and starts up again, the sixteenth noise has disappeared.

His hand rests lightly on the wheel while he drives. When he breaks a chain of cigarettes and needs to light up once more, he passes the cigarette to whoever is sitting next to him. Since the windows of the truck let in a swift current of air at the top and the sides – the rubber strips have disappeared in places – the operation of lighting a match in the moving truck is not easy, and I usually pass it on to Gyanseng. Sui drives, for the most part, gently; this contrasts with the violence of his gear changes. On mountainous stretches he steers with a sensitive adeptness that is enjoyable to watch.

He and Gyanseng get along well. They do not speak much. Gyanseng is a little sick of road travel. Sometimes when we are in a transport yard overnight, Sui tells him to sleep in the truck to guard it. Gyanseng grumbles about the cold and discomfort but complies: it is vital the driver gets a good night's rest. When I try to insist on taking over on alternate nights I am over-ruled. In matters relating to the truck, the driver is dictator.

Unlike almost all Han Chinese I have met (including many educated at university), Sui is not Han-chauvinist. He neither looks down on nor up to the Tibetans. He is not interested in their culture: despite the fact that he has lived in Lhasa for fifteen years he speaks almost no Tibetan. Yet he has a way of treating people as individuals rather than as representatives of types, that precludes any sense of cultural superiority. His friends and acquaintances along the route are Han and Tibetan, though naturally the Tibetans are restricted to those who can speak Chinese. Unlike some of his fellow drivers and army buddies he has not once indicated any dislike of Lhasa or of Tibet or of Tibetans. For him it is not 'New Zealand' but home.

He reads omnivorously: newspapers when he can get them, Xiao San's comic books, novels, short stories in magazines, instruction booklets. 'Poetry,' he tells me, 'is pointless. I can never understand what poets are trying to get at – or why they bother to say things the way they do.' He describes his school life during the Cultural Revolution. 'We never studied, never did anything. I was interested in books, but any reading I did I did without guidance. My sister's a doctor – you'll meet her at Germu – but that sort of thing is completely closed off to me. I am too old now for higher studies. Besides, I don't have the qualifications.'

'Do you regret it?' I ask.

'Yes, sometimes, of course. But what's the point? Even if I didn't accept the way things are, what could I do? And this is not a bad life anyway. I'm lucky as such things go. The one problem with the job is that I'm rarely with my family.'

Together with this resignation comes a certain savvy, a street-smartness that enables Sui to find his way about the system, to utilise its flexibilities, to withdraw when effort is useless, to know when and how to bargain, whom to speak with when in trouble, how to get a concession here, a few litres of petrol (when necessary) there. When my luggage fell off the truck he did not spend time thinking about the best course of action; when we realised someone had absconded with it, he looked ahead sufficiently far to ask the identifying witness to come with us to Liuyuan. When, past midnight, we arrived in Dunhuang, he combined argument and pleasantry to get us a room in a yard that we had been told was full. Wherever we are, he looks out for gifts or good bargains for himself and for his friends. He is a generous man. In a sense the hard-bitten side of his nature inspires as much confidence as his patent goodheartedness.

The landscape is so spectacular that I seem hardly to have noticed our more mundane activities today. We have stopped for oil and water and diesel several times, but haven't eaten anything except lunch at a truck depot (bean-curd, and rice, and a kind of squid-like thing I couldn't identify). I felt like eating some grapes but the egg had got squashed into them in transit. From time to time we stop at a checkpost or fuel station where one or two families have lived in isolation from the rest of humanity for perhaps twenty years.

This Chaidam Basin must be among the loneliest parts of the world. Sui invariably asks the old men who are stationed at such places what they would like him to bring for them the next time he is going through. He sells them a watermelon or two at cost price, or gives them some present he has brought along – a book perhaps, or a pair of shoes. They are always very pleased to see him. Cigarettes are offered all around; Sui must smoke a couple of packs of Da Qian Men a day. We are making good distance today, for the first time. By the time we're at the salt lake,

Sui needs another rest, and sleeps for half an hour at the house of one of his endless wayside acquaintances. Before moving on, we fill a few gunny bags with rock salt we shovel out of the surface of the lake; all of us get down to digging and hauling the stuff. A segment of railway track approaches Germu from the east, and we dig for salt beside it. It must be an eerie sight by the light of the moon.

The night is so clear that the sky looks stuffed with stars, busier than I can remember ever having seen it. Gyanseng, who has been quiet all day, starts singing in Tibetan. Xiao San's headache is better and his temper is worse. I continue talking to Sui, who is in a meditative mood.

Sui thinks that young people nowadays are disturbed and selfish, and blames it on the viciousness of the Cultural Revolution, during which they were encouraged to turn against their parents and teachers and everyone in authority, and instead to follow the (prevailing) message of Mao. All decency died during that time, he says, and half the cultural heritage of China – books, temples, works of art – was destroyed. People now care only for themselves. And as for their skills, even their literacy – no-one really studied anything in school, that is if they went to school at all. All day they had to recite and discuss the quotations of the Chairman, as if that was the totality of all knowledge. You should have seen the *People's Daily* during those days, he says – red headlines across the front page: 'We will endlessly adore the red sun in our lives, Chairman Mao' – and who can blame the kids for being influenced by such ever-present propaganda?

'Was there nothing good in the Cultural Revolution at all?' I ask. 'Some people mention that the only time they got to travel, to see their country, was when they were Red Guards. And they say it cut down on the worst abuses of bureaucracy.'

'Well, I suppose that's true, though I'm not too sure about the bureaucracy.' He does not speak for a while, then goes on. 'Some good things came out of it, as they do out of every disaster. I learned a lot of things about life, and about how people behave: about how far, for instance, you could count on even your best friends to stick by you in times of trouble. Sometimes people wanted to but they didn't dare help. They feared for themselves and for their families.'

Very late, at one o'clock at night, we arrive in Germu. The people at the desk at the Transport Yard are surly; in particular the gatekeeper, who is arrogant and suspicious in the extreme. I am given a bureaucratic run-around when I am so sleepy that I can hardly talk. Finally we are given a room, and the manager appears, apologising in the name of international friendship. It is hardly his fault, and he has been woken up as well. I am asleep within minutes.

At 3.15 comes a knock on the door. I wake up, but ignore it until it becomes too insistent to ignore. 'Who is it?' I ask. 'Police,' comes the reply. I get out of bed and open the door. A police officer in white uniform and cap looks in at us severely. (By this time Sui too has woken up.) 'Why didn't you open up when I first knocked?' he asks. 'We were asleep,' I say. 'Is anything the matter?'

'Kindly come to the office with me.'

'Can't we do this tomorrow?' I ask plaintively.

'I am afraid not. There are some questions we need to ask you.'

I pull on a sweater and a pair of warm socks, and trying to conquer my sleepiness and conceal my agitation I follow the officer across the yard. In the office the gatekeeper looks at me with the contentment of a spider observing a struggling fly.

'Sit here,' says the officer, indicating a bench opposite a table. I do as I am told.

He looks at the register. 'What is your name? Your Chinese name?'

'Xie Binlang. And yours?' I ask conversationally.

He ignores this. 'What is your unit?'

'Nanjing University.'

'Oh. And do they know you are here in Germu?'

'I very much doubt it.'

'Are you here to do research?'

'No. I am here to . . .'

'Let me ask the questions. You are not here to do research. Are you here for any other special purpose?'

'Special purpose? What do you mean?'

'I mean . . . on a study trip, something your university has sanctioned.'

'No, I'm just travelling.'

77

'And how did you get here?'

'I hitch-hiked.'

'Hitch-hiked.' He chews this over. 'You have your travel pass?'

'Yes. Here it is.'

'I see that Germu is not on it.'

'Yes, but Lhasa is, and I am just passing through Germu. It's like stopping at Shanghai station overnight on the way to Nanjing. You don't need it on your pass.'

'I am afraid it is not quite the same thing. If you had spent the night outside the town it would not have been our concern, but once you enter the municipal precincts you are in Germu proper and you should have reported to us immediately you arrived.'

'But we arrived at one o'clock in the morning, and would never have been able to find you. Anyway I planned to report to the police in the morning, at a reasonable hour.'

He looks at me as I say the last words. 'Mr Xie, I do not think you realise that this is not something to be taken lightly. Regulations are regulations.' (*Guiding shi guiding* – ah, how often I have heard this phrase.)

I look as apologetic as I can. He scrutinises the travel pass. 'Where is Lhasa marked on this pass?'

'On the opposite page, under Endorsements.'

'Ah, yes. And you say you hitch-hiked. Why didn't you fly directly to Lhasa by plane?'

'I couldn't afford it. Plane tickets are twice as expensive for foreigners as for Chinese.'

'Yes; it's a *guiding*. And do you have permission to hitch-hike?'

'Well, under Means of Transport Permitted, you will see '*Qiche*',' I state. *Qiche* is a Chinese word that includes cars, trucks, buses, vans, jeeps, etc. (literally, 'steam cart'). Above it, in English, is written the translation, 'car', but I argue to myself that the Chinese is primary, and since we used minibuses on the university trip, I should interpret *qiche* in its wider sense. I am glad he does not read English.

'It says on this pass that you are an Indian citizen. Do you plan to go to any border areas?'

'Well, I hope to go on after Lhasa to Nepal and then return home. I will not cross any Sino-Indian border.'

'Could you show me your passport?'

I hand it over. As I do, a colour photograph of the family – Papa, Mama, Aradhana, myself – drops out of it onto the table. The officer looks at it – at my father's kurta and pyjama, my mother's tika and sari, my dishevelled hair, my sister's slight frown as she looks into the sun – and, for the first time, smiles.

'Your family?'

'Yes.'

His whole attitude changes. 'It's a very nice photograph. You're going home for the holidays?'

'Yes.'

'Have you been away for long?'

'It's been three years since the last time I was home.' I wonder about him. Sometimes Chinese officials in outlying provinces are away from their families for longer.

'You've been in China three years?'

'No, just this past year. Before that I was in America.'

'Do you study there?'

'Yes, economics and demography. I'm doing some field research this year in the countryside near Nanjing.'

'Ah, both our countries have so many problems.' He seems lost in thought for a while. 'Well, it is late. I think you can go now.'

'Do I need to fill any registration forms?'

'No, no. You can do all that in the morning. No need to come to the police station. We'll send the forms along.'

'Well, thank you.'

'Not at all. Have a good sleep, Mr Xie. And a good journey.'

8

Germu:
a wilderness town

After a breakfast of cold *mantou* and a visit to the office to sign the police forms, I return to our room and read up on Qinghai in my little vade-mecum atlas of Chinese maps.

Qinghai, 700,000 square kilometres in area, is considerably larger than France, and has a population of about four million. Even this fact does not give one a clear picture of just how sparse the population is over most of Qinghai, since almost all of it is concentrated in a small eastern pocket, where arable farming is possible. Xining, the provincial capital, lies here. Germu, in the centre of the province, is surrounded by an almost barren basin to the north and an equally barren plateau to the south. A few army settlements dot the main road from Liuyuan to Lhasa. These sometimes double as trading posts for Kazakh and Tibetan herdsmen.

The Chaidam Basin, which we have just crossed, lies at an altitude of between 1,800 and 2,700 metres. After Germu, as we continue south, we will rise suddenly onto the Qinghai–Tibet plateau, to altitudes of 4,000–5,000 metres: to thin air, sharp sunshine by day and intense cold by night.

Qinghai's population, through both natural increase and Han settlement, has risen sharply since Liberation. Pastoral farming could be further developed. There are rich resources of oil in the west, and both coal and salt along the route we have just travelled. The salt lake we crossed is the second largest in the world, and contains almost pure sodium chloride more than ten metres thick over an area of 100 square kilometres. There is therefore scope for the development of a chemical industry. Oil exploration is continuing with international assistance in the northwest corner of Qinghai. As for Germu itself, which has burgeoned up out of almost nothing in the last twenty years, it seems to be an important military station of no great present economic significance.

An acquaintance of Sui's comes into the room whilst we are reading. He had shared his room yesterday with two men from Sichuan, and now they have made off with all his luggage, including his clothes. (A friend lent him the ones he's wearing now.) The police, he tells us, arrived promptly and have alerted the checkpoints. As there are only three roads leading out of Germu, they are confident that the thieves will not be able to get away. All this leads me to ask Sui what he thinks will happen to the man who took my luggage. Sui thinks that if this is his first offence, the police will probably take a lenient view of things, as it was not a planned theft, more a sudden yielding to temptation. But they will almost certainly send a letter to his unit, and he will be put on probation for a while.

Gyanseng, full of optimism, goes to buy a plane ticket. I go off to buy cigarettes. Sui has taken excellent care of me all along the journey, and has refused payment for many of the expenses, meals, for example, that we should have shared. He is running low on cigarettes, and having suffered last night on account of my foreignness, I decide to take advantage of it today to get him some good ones.

I walk around the town. The stores and public buildings have a tedious architectural similarity to those in Nanjing or Xian or Lanzhou or Turfan. I have never seen so many off-duty soldiers walking along the streets. Twenty years ago there were a few tents here, nothing more. Now it is a flourishing small town with a free market in mostly bruised vegetables, a movie theatre, a bank, a bookstore, and signs in four languages – Chinese, Tibetan, Kazakh and Mongolian. Anyone who is not a soldier looks like an alien; I less so than most because of my conventional blue clothing (I have left my conspicuous backpack at the Transport Yard). Two Kazakhs ride into town on white horses. A vendor selling overripe grapes watches indifferently as a thick crust of flies settles over them. I ask him where I can get cigarettes; he directs me to a food and provisions store beyond the bookshop.

As I stand before the counter, I notice a brand of cigarettes Sui has mentioned he likes. I ask for a carton, whereupon the saleswoman looks at me as though I were mad. 'You can't buy those.'

'Oh, why not?' I ask, handing over a ten yuan note of funny money. Unlike the sheepskin vendor at Turfan, her eyes do not light up.

'What's this? Is this money?' she asks.

By now a small crowd has gathered around. Someone takes a close look at the note. 'It's money all right – says "Bank of China" on it. But it also says "Foreign Exchange Certificate". He must be a foreigner.'

A foreigner. No one can remember there ever having been a foreigner in Germu. What is to be done about his request and his currency? Doesn't he know the regulations? These good cigarettes can only be bought with special coupons, issued mainly to army personnel.

'Where can I get these coupons?' I ask.

'Down at the bank. You could probably convince them, but then, of course, today's Sunday.'

'Couldn't you just let me have a few packs?' I ask. 'I'll be leaving Germu this evening, and Lhasa is a long way away. It's a "special circumstance".'

But apparently not special enough. I go out, disappointed, to find the bank. It's empty except for a couple of employees clearing up leftover work at their desks.

'Sunday,' one says as I enter.

In pidgin Chinese I explain my plight, casually resting my left arm on the counter.

The combination of the speech and the watch is enough to convince them that I am a foreigner. (I have noticed that in China, the better your Chinese, the worse the treatment you get from officials: the first few sentences should be delivered haltingly, in a thick accent, and as ungrammatically as possible.) But regulations are regulations, and even here I cannot get the coupons today. They are, however, willing to take me to the manager's house. This lies, as is quite often the case in China, in a compound behind his place of work. He is surprised but interested to see me; his wife and daughter come into the room to ask me a few autobiographical details. While we talk, the manager sends for the accountant. The accountant looks grave. 'Sunday, you know.'

'Well,' says the manager eventually, 'why don't I just talk directly to my good friend, the manager of the store?'

We walk back up the street to the store. The bank manager enters by a small gate at the side of the store: we find ourselves in another small compound, where the store manager lives.

The situation is explained again. The store manager examines my funny money. We re-enter the store. A few words are exchanged with the saleswoman, who shrugs her shoulders indifferently and takes a couple of cartons from the shelf. What the management decide to allow or disallow is their business.

Feeling gratitude to these people, and just a slight twinge of guilt for having done this 'through the back door', as the Chinese put it, I walk back towards the truck. Sui is leaning against the door, reading a newspaper. 'Where is Gyanseng?' I ask. 'Oh, he's gone back to the Transport Station,' replies Sui. 'He couldn't get a ticket. Where have you been? You've certainly taken your time. My sister will be waiting: they've asked us to lunch.'

Xiao San's father and mother greet us at the door. They are not at all surprised to see me – Sui must have told them that we would all be coming – but they are curious, and so for the first half hour or so my mouth is occupied with tea and toffee and answers to a series of questions. They are both doctors: there is a diagnostic flavour to their interrogation. Xiao San's mother is a small strong-willed personality who keeps strict order in the family. Xiao San is subdued in her presence, and Sui comments on his unwonted politeness. Xiao San's father is a thin and gentle man who has a nervous, hospitable manner. In between questions he searches through the toffees in the tin for particularly good ones, which he then presses on me. My teacup is continually replenished, and a fresh cigarette proffered before I have finished the last one. 'If there is anything you want, please ask us. Anything,' he says. 'We live in very poor conditions. I am so sorry.'

In fact, the two long rooms plus small yard and shack outside, are spacious by Chinese standards. The tall rooms, connected by a door, are of brick, and their cross-section is like that of a railway tunnel. During the hottest days of the year this must keep them cool, although the heat from the stove during the winter must rise straight up to the ceiling. Lunch is prepared by Xiao San's mother, and is superb. Throughout the meal I am told that the food is very poor, and that my Chinese is very good, both of which make about equal sense.

There are four sons in the family, two of whom are away in college. (I sometimes detect a slight unease on Sui's part around his well-educated sister and brother-in-law, especially when they talk about their two eldest sons.) The younger ones – Xiao San ('Little Third') and Xiao Si ('Little Fourth') are still with the family. Xiao Si is nine years old and so full of enthusiasm about everything that he breathes in hasty gasps between long paragraphs of rapid speech. He is telling me how wonderful Germu is. I must see all the sights, including the airport. In point of fact, though, this is a town where there is singularly little to see that is not of a military nature. I am reminded of when I was his age, and thought even Patna (where I lived) an exciting town, and a climb to the top of the Golghar granary an adventure to be savoured for days.

Sui disappears after lunch to perform his postponed tasks. 'I'll be back by six o'clock,' he says. At the door he turns. 'Well, maybe six-thirty.' By now I know better than to trust his sense of time, and expect him back at eight. For my afternoon nap, or *xiuxi*, Xiao San's father, holding the toffee tin, leads me to the tiny annexe in the yard. It is just large enough for a bed and a desk. Flies buzz around inside, a truck starts up outside. Chickens cluck in a coop outside the door and a dog barks at the gate. Xiao Si and his friends suck iced lollies, and play a form of hopscotch on the dusty street, yelling vigorously when anyone makes a doubtful jump. I lie down on the narrow but comfortable bed and rest my head on the towelled pillow.

As I listen to the sounds outside, it strikes me that although I know a certain amount about the language, literature and history of China, I am appallingly ignorant about the songs, the lullabies, the nursery rhymes, the street games of children, the riddles; all the things that are most important in the childhood of Chinese people. Chinese language courses do not include this; indeed, how could they be expected to? Yet without such things one cannot understand the wealth of references made to a common past, the casual assumptions of shared experiences that lie behind conversation in any language. It is like knowing *Macbeth* without knowing 'Three Blind Mice', or the *Ramayana* without 'Chanda Mama'.

As I doze off to the soporific drone of flies, I dream of being back at Stanford University. I have been crowned chairman of the Asian Languages department, and have inaugurated a six-month intensive course in Chinese. Each week corresponds to a year in the life of the Chinese child. For the first week my students lie around on cots in the classroom, making various burbling noises while I and two other teachers talk in Chinese to each other. The students throw tantrums, but not as often as the American baby. They are wheeled about the campus in prams, and swathed in over-thick padded clothes, just as Chinese infants are: they always remind me of overheated dumplings. In my totalitarian scheme of things, my students are sung to sleep at regular intervals with lullabies. The second week, a few elementary words are taught to them: 'baba', 'mama', and so on. At mealtimes or when taken for a walk they are expected to display a proper curiosity for the names of objects, though, in conformity with the Mayonnaise Principle, the intake of new lexical information has to be controlled. (The Mayonnaise Principle states that learning a language is like making mayonnaise: add too much at once and the mixture will separate out.) Slowly, through the compressed years, the students come into contact with nursery rhymes, written characters, simple comic books, schoolchildren's slang and sneers, buying and selling vocabulary, the use of chopsticks, pen, brush and abacus. They now participate in adult conversation, read short stories, perform songs for visiting Party dignitaries and foreign guests, drink endless cups of hot water from brightly-coloured thermos flasks, etc. As they rush through their adolescence and early adulthood, I introduce political thought, history, literature, bureaucracy, slogans and obscenities. By the end of the six-month course, in their twenty-sixth year, my students (all of whom are about to be married off and/or be sent off to the post that has been allocated to them) have some idea of the experience of their Chinese peers. They are just thanking me when Xiao

San's father enters, bearing peanuts and boiled sweets: 'I thought you might be hungry.'

After he leaves I try to re-enter my dream, but cannot. Eventually, I settle down to another one where I am trying to feed cigarette coupons to a yak. When I wake up again it is dark. Sui has not returned. I join the others for dinner.

Later, a friend of the family, a bike mechanic, drops in for a chat. Sui's brother-in-law is a surgeon, but there is no sense of social superiority in their conversation. One of the topics they discuss is salaries, but the fact that one gets 50 yuan and the other 105 yuan does not lead to resentment. The bicycle mechanic has independent views on politics. 'I read what everyone has to say, and make up my own mind,' he says. 'I don't subscribe to any party, and I suppose it's as well I'm a mechanic, because I don't have to get involved in politics and faction.' He could have gone to university when he was young but for 'family circumstances'. He knows a fair amount about the current Indian political scene, through what he modestly calls 'erratic' reading in the newspapers. He was in Lhasa in the 1950s and remembers when Nehru sent an elephant as a gift to Tibet.

Sui returns around eleven o'clock, hungry and exhausted. His sister cooks for him, and he sits on a stool in the kitchen without saying a word. We are leaving tonight, late as it is. In part I am responsible for this, since staying another day means reporting to the police again. Xiao San helps load the truck. 'Well then, I'm off,' says Sui to his sister. 'Have a good journey,' she says, smiling. They do not exchange a hug but the parting is nevertheless affectionate. She stands out on the street until the truck moves away.

I have noticed that the Hans are in general a very reserved people. They do not wear bright clothes. The slightest non-conformist behaviour is stared at and commented upon. Men and women maintain a strict restraint in their attitude towards each other: they do not feel comfortable touching, even in a purely friendly way. Yet the sight of two men or two women walking down the street with their arms around each other's shoulders or waists is as common in China as it is in India. The great Chinese poets have written far more frequently about friendship than they have about romantic love. This is one area where the Han reserve is least apparent; another is the love that parents lavish on their young children.

We arrive at the Transport Yard in a few minutes. Sui rushes about looking for Gyanseng, shouting loudly enough to wake anyone within a few hundred yards' radius. Gyanseng appears after five minutes of this. He is dishevelled and angry. He clutches his bag and glares at Sui. 'You said you'd be here by five-thirty,' he says. 'Then we were to go over to your sister's place to load the truck. Do you know what time it is now?'

Sui is appeasing. 'I should have told you. I should have told you. I was delayed. You know how it is.'

Gyanseng's anger moves him to speak at length, for once. 'Delayed. I waited until ten o'clock before booking myself in for another night. One yuan and twenty-five cents. I had just got to sleep when you started bellowing. No, I'm going back to my room; let's leave tomorrow in the morning.'

'Come on, Gyanseng, I'm sorry about this. We can't spend another night here. Lao Xie here has told the police he'll be in Germu for less than twenty-four hours. We should leave before midnight. We'll take a break on the way and rest for an hour or so.' Sui himself looks very tired.

Gyanseng is mollified. We get back into the truck. With Xiao San gone there should be a little more space; but Sui has placed a number of additional bags and boxes at our feet, and these restore the equilibrium of discomfort. No sooner are we in the truck than Gyanseng leans on my shoulder and falls asleep. I have rested well this afternoon and do not need it much. But Sui, who has slept least of all of us in the last few days and whose face is drawn with tiredness, has four hours of difficult driving ahead until we climb to the next Transport Yard, at the rim of the vast escarpment of the Qinghai–Tibet plateau.

After two hours of tiresome driving – the road twists and turns as the truck strains up the edge of the plateau – we stop by a reservoir in the hills. We huddle together in the truck cabin and sleep for an hour. The sound of a high wind and a roaring stream forms the backdrop to our slumbers. Sui wakes up and drives like a robot until we arrive, at 4.30 in the morning, at a Transport Yard located in the middle of nowhere. The place is desolate, the accommodation shack-like and filthy, but we're happy to be able to stretch out.

From time to time I am concerned that this trip will get Sui into some sort of trouble with his work-unit. Last night I was anxious about him. But as incident follows incident, and no-one – neither the police at Liuyuan, nor the officials at the Transport Yard at Germu – cares in the slightest about Sui's role in my journey, so I feel more and more at ease. Whenever he is asked, Sui says that the lift was arranged by a member of the Public Security Bureau, and that is always that. My papers were examined, at the beginning, by Quzha, and later, by the Liuyuan police. By now I realise that all truckers give lifts to friends, or strangers, and that there is nothing unusual about my method of travel other than the fact that I am not Chinese.

9

Southern Qinghai:
the cold plateau

10th August I wake up a little after light. Standing at the gate of the Transport Yard I look up and down the empty road. There are no houses, no people other than those manning the yard itself or the gas station a few hundred metres down. A stream flows beside the road. Beyond it a gently convex range of hills stands, covered with snow. The air is crisp but sparse. The sun's rays at this altitude are fierce. When we hit the road again, the part of my arm outside the truck gets sunburnt within an hour. There are no signs of humanity here, at the halfway mark between Liuyuan and Lhasa. Every few kilometres or so, a large and very glossy raven sits perched on a telegraph pole, karking desolately.

Sui's remarks about the rigours of the journey beyond Germu struck forcibly home this morning. Breakfast at the truckers' yard was a few mouldering peanuts and a piece of steamed bread, or *mantou*, gritty inside and slimy outside. Lunch, at a small settlement where we arrive in the early afternoon, is much the same. As it happens, I am no longer hungry. A splitting headache, which Sui attributes to the altitude, makes all thought of food repellent. The suddenness of this attack is unsettling, as I had just been congratulating myself on adapting with no ill effects to the thinner air. The truck jolts along the road, which is no more than a bumpy track. I feel my brains bursting through my skull.

The Qinghai–Tibet plateau is marked by three main ranges stretching from east to west. In between lie high plains crossed by streams and rivers. The northernmost range is the Kunlun, almost at the northern edge of the plateau. The southernmost range is the Himalayas. About midway between the two lies the Tangula Range which marks the border between Qinghai and Tibet.

The road climbs to the Kunlun Pass, over 4,000 metres high; the small valley we have been moving along grows broader as we rise. Soon the land is marsh-like and very lightly curved. The stream is irresolute and meanders along the slope. The rise is so slight that if it were not for the stone markers, I would not have known when we had crossed the highest point.

'How are you feeling?' asks Sui, conversationally.

'Terrible.'

'Really?' he laughs. 'That bad?'

'Yes.'

'Why don't you eat something? Here's a *mantou*.'

'No.'

'It'll get better, you know. You'll get used to it.'

'Oh?'

'I did warn you that it would be bad after Germu.'

'Yes.'

Sui pauses, then tries again. 'You know, they used to say that this area, the Kunlun Mountains, was the home of heavenly spirits.'

'Oh.'

'What do you think of the scenery?' he asks.

'It's all right.'

Actually, even through my unsociable fog of pain I can tell that the scenery is very beautiful. At the foot of the pass, on the southern side, a broad stream flows across the plain. It is brick-red with sediment, redder even than the silt-laden Colorado River during its course through the Grand Canyon. Near the stream a herd of deer stand grazing. When the truck passes close by them, they bound swiftly, but unhurriedly, away.

In this season the normally arid plateau is a squelchy mass of mud. The army is working on laying down a metalled road; but in the interim this merely makes things worse. All along the road are signs: 'Detour: Strictly Prohibited to Continue Along Road'. The improvised detours lead straight into the waterlogged plains. Several times we get stuck in this mud, and have to get out and push. When other trucks are in trouble we try to haul them out. One in particular, with a load of eight tons – it is carrying steel rods – has clung limpet-like to us for help; our cargo of insulating material is only three tons, so we have energy to spare. It is beginning to sleet, and the most treacherous section of the road is just ahead. Further delay is dangerous since with every minute the ground becomes more and more of a paste. But the eight-ton truck is honking pathetically for assistance; it is difficult to ignore its distress.

We flounder onwards after extricating our fellow vehicle, but it is too late. We no longer bump along the slithery ruts of the track but are instead sucked in by a red slush that covers half the wheels. It is now raining harder. Sui curses and we get out to push, but it's no use. He gets out his spade and digs out some mud from in front of the wheels and tries the first gear. Then he digs out mud from behind the wheels and tries the reverse gear. But we are in a slippery trough, already half-filled with rain. The wheels go around, the air is filled with black diesel fumes, but the truck does not move forward.

The vehicle in front of us is now stuck, too, not to mention the eight-ton truck behind. Other trucks that tried to get off the main track have got bogged down in other parts of the plain, and now dot the landscape like squat ducks shot down in mud.

From somewhere quite far off (it seems) Gyanseng's and Sui's voices seep into my befuddled mind.

'Looks bad.'

'Problem is, there's no drainage on the plain.'

'The sun's low, too.'

'Yes, it won't evaporate off.'

'Looks like we're . . .'

'. . . Stuck here for the night. Yes. Just hope it doesn't rain again before morning.'

'I should have tried harder to get a plane ticket to Germu.'

'What's done is done. Wrap yourself up well; it'll be cold tonight. You too, Lao Xie.'

There is nothing to do but sit and read. Gyanseng hums to himself. Sui reads a short story in a magazine; he bursts out laughing from time to time. I'm reading Naipaul's book in short snatches, putting it down every few minutes to nurse my headache. I can't help feeling distressed by what he has to say about India, but it is better than a hundred books of calmer but less insightful analysis. It is a complex, driven book – it forces me either into agreement or argument. Finally the effort of reading becomes too painful. Then the effort of thinking becomes too painful. I look at Sui and Gyanseng in wonder: they are totally unaffected by the paucity of the air.

The clouds have gone, and now the sun has sunk; the thin atmosphere gives up its warmth completely. I shiver, regretting that I have not brought my 'Lei Feng' cap with me. (This cap, similar to the one habitually worn by a much-propagandised soldier-worker hero, has a thick crown and heavy earflaps.) And I haven't even brought my sleeping-bag.

Romantic retrospect aside, the night spent in the truck is distinctly unpleasant. We are cramped and cold. The much-vaunted heating of the truck is ineffectual. The wind prises through the cracks in the sides of the windows, and penetrates us to the bone. My feet are moist in my shoes, yet to take my socks off is to chill my feet even further. We take every warm item of clothing out of our bags and swaddle ourselves into immobility. The sheepskin on the seat cuts out a bit of the cold rising from below. We share a blanket and Sui, before he goes off to sleep, makes sure I get a generous part of this. He then drops off to sleep, and tugs it away. He jockeys for space, and I am forced to lean forward. He begins to snore. To make it all worse, both he and Gyanseng sleeptalk. They have told me before that I do, too, but I've never noticed it. What I do notice, however, late at night, with my two territorially acquisitive companions wedging me forwards, is that I have started talking to myself: naming the constellations I can see move across the mud-stained windscreen, interviewing myself, reciting odd snatches of poetry. I also notice that I am hungry, which is curious, because during the day I was not; and itchy, which is to be expected after so much unwashed travel; and sleepy, though I cannot sleep for cold and headache and discomfort; and, alas, bored out of my mind.

When things get really bad, I imagine myself in a darkened room, up to my shoulders in a tub of hot water, with a glass of Grand Marnier beside me and the second movement of Mozart's Clarinet Quintet sounding gently in my ears. This voluptuous vision, rather than making my present condition seem even more insupportable, actually enables me to escape for a while from the complaints of my suffering body.

11th August   The sky lightens slowly, but the whole plain is lost in mist. The red ruts of the road can be seen a little way into the mist, but no trucks are visible. Engine noises and peoples' voices filter through to us. We do not even bother to start up. There is no way we can get out unless the ground dries up.

Yesterday, in the evening, we noticed a huge roadbuilding vehicle with caterpillar tracks sitting in a mound about two kilometres down the road. The idea of remaining immobile for who knows how long – a few hours? A few days? – impels me to make an effort. When Sui asks me where the hell I think I'm going, I tell him I'm off to fetch help; I get down from the truck with torch in hand and take a few hesitant steps into the mud.

The road itself is too muddy, so I walk off it, trying not to stray too far into the mist. Small, round, compact and furry rats run around, darting in and out of holes. White-eared rabbits also leap confusingly about: they are clearly visible one moment; but one jump later they have completely disappeared into the fog. I pause for a few minutes. I am exhausted by the small expenditure of effort required just to walk. Finally, I arrive at the enormous vehicle; the man who drives it has just started up. He looks at me in puzzlement.

'I wonder if you could help us,' I ask. 'Our truck is stuck in the mud a little way down the road, and I do not think we will be able to get out by ourselves. I am a foreigner, on my way to Lhasa. I should be there as soon as possible. My papers expire soon.

The driver responds to this shameless attempt at persuasion and pressure by saying, 'Sure. I can help you. In fact I want to help you. But you will have to ask my *lingdao* in the road-repair camp for permission before I start.'

'Where is the camp?'

'A few kilometres down the road. There are tents on the ground. You can't miss it.'

'Thanks.'

'Listen, I'll drive down to where the trucks are stuck. But I can't begin work without permission. O.K.?'

I continue the misty trek through the slush. A shoe gets sucked off into the mud; I get down on my knees to pull it out. I pause to catch my breath before venturing further. By the time I reach the tents I am exhausted.

The road-repair *lingdao* are astonished to see me stumble in out of the fog. I have brought my papers along, which they examine with interest. They give me hot green tea with sugar in it. The *lingdao*, willing to help, get into another caterpillar-treaded vehicle and we head back to the stretch of the road where the trucks, incapable as dinosaurs, lie sunk beneath their own weight in the soft earth. The other vehicle has joined us; the two mammoth machines, aided by a troop of spade-wielding roadworkers, dig up and flatten down the road. They then haul the trucks out one by one. With a reluctant squelch the mud relinquishes us too.

We move on down the road, followed closely by our eight-ton friend. The fog has cleared, and the road, though still horrendously uneven, is drier than before.

The climate has become markedly monsoonal as we have moved further south. Late in the afternoon clouds gather again and there is a hailstorm followed by a short but tremendous burst of rain. Again, like yesterday, this is followed by clear skies. Luckily we are travelling on less treacherous terrain, and manage to advance without getting stuck. We are in time to get shelter for the night. Late in the evening we roll into the settlement of Tuotuohe, refuel, and check into the Transport Yard. Needless to say, the food is almost inedible. We nibble biscuits and raisins, but Sui also buys a bowl of soup, alive with odious globs of pork-fat. This he swallows with a phlegmatic air, as if he were merely refuelling the truck.

'Lao Sui, how can you eat that stuff?' I ask.

Sui looks at me, amused. 'It's all right.'

'I couldn't get it down if I wanted to.'

'I've eaten worse.'

'But . . . lumps of fat, with bits of skin and hair still on them?'

'You know,' says Sui, 'I can guarantee that if you were to drink a bowl of this soup, you'd feel much better. You haven't eaten anything for the last few days. Fat's very good: it has lots of energy.'

I am not persuaded.

By now I have the worst headache I have had for years, with fever and nausea thrown in. This is the worst road – if it can be called that – that I've ever travelled on for any length, so jolty – when passable – that my head feels as though there's liquid inside, sloshing around uncontrollably. I am interested in nothing but drawing my quilt over my head and going to sleep.

Gyanseng, on the other hand, whose taciturnity has so far made conversation difficult, now bursts out into monologues on odd subjects, like tea, or Lhasa. As we approach Tibet, a latent loquaciousness begins to emerge. This takes the form of singing or humming, interspersed with explanations of the songs. They are usually Tibetan folk songs, but his repertoire also includes a number of Chinese popular songs and others, alas, well-beloved all over China, such as 'Do Re Mi', 'Jingle Bells' and 'Red River Valley'. When Gyanseng is most content, he sings out of tune. Because he is usually so self-contained, it is only at times like these that I recall that he is the youngest of us three.

12th August   Today was dominated by army camps and yaks.

We stopped at a number of army camps (either collections of tents or more permanent barracks) yesterday and the day before, but today Sui has a field day.

Many of the soldiers in the camps have been to Pakistani-held Kashmir to work on the Karakoram Highway. Some were stationed in Gilgit. They don't seem to have had much social contact with the Pakistanis, though. One man, who lived there for five years, never once ate Pakistani food; they lived separately, and everything, including food, was brought from China. They picked up a certain amount of Urdu during their working days (*Kya hal hai?*, *baitho*, *dost*, *subedar*, *gaari*) which they now eagerly practise on me. Everyone is extremely friendly. We are now not far from the Tangula Range; the soldiers insist that once we cross the 5,400 metre Tangula Pass into Tibet my altitude sickness will disappear.

When the frequency of Sui's friendly wayside halts increases dramatically, Gyanseng and I develop a camaraderie of the oppressed which makes the waiting tolerable. We are both eager to be in Lhasa soon, and Sui's indifference is tiresome. Sometimes we just boycott the visits, and remain in the truck. If we had thought that this would make him abridge his visits, we soon realise that it has no such effect. For Sui, unlike us, this is not just a journey: it is a style of life. He spends more time on the road than in Lhasa, and it is the contacts and acquaintances along the route that lend relief and flavour to his hours behind the wheel.

While Sui is engaged with another of his endless cronies (and has actually persuaded my erstwhile ally to accompany him), I sit in the truck and look out over the plateau, which is now covered with a sparse growth of grass. I am shaken out of my lassitude by the appearance of a herd of black, thick-haired yaks who emerge from behind a slight rise up ahead. They stop about a hundred metres up the road and graze calmly, lowing and snorting now and then. They are huge beasts, and have a solemnity becoming to animals their size; not so the little yaks, however, who run around, alarmingly playful and ebullient. Some of them stand in the middle of the road. When a truck passes every ten minutes or so, they stare at it in shock until it is almost upon them, then kick up their heels in panic and scamper off into the plain.

Yaks look like Pekinese dogs or willow trees in the way that their hair sprouts downward off them. For all their largeness and solemnity, they are friendly beasts. I would like to see them at closer range sometime.

We begin to climb the great Tangula Range late in the afternoon. A zone of flowers – buttercups and cornflowers among them – carpets the banks of the swift snow-fed stream. Here, too, there are raucous and splendid ravens. On the far bank of the twining stream a green hill rises sharply, a stone corral on its slope. Two horses and some sheep graze there. A herd of yaks obstructs the road but disperses indignantly when Sui presses the horn.

At Yanshipin, on the bank of this stream, is a ferry. The tall green hills here are riven by serrated ribs of red rock. The people have a darker appearance and squarer features than the Hans: they are Tibetans. Men and sheep cross on the little boat, which shuttles back and forth along a cable suspended above the stream. Sui stops the truck. Gyanseng and I look at each other. 'I'll just be a minute,' says Sui, disappearing into a friend's house.

When he returns, an hour later, it is almost sunset. Our route takes us straight into the low sun. The atrocious glare merges with my atrocious headache to give this beautiful landscape the quality of a scene in a nightmare. What's more, I cannot tell if the nightmare is in colour or in black-and-white. The antics of the light cause grass and water to turn suddenly from green and blue to black and silver. Round a corner the sun strikes directly again, and the scene is again green and blue. As with the Kunlun Pass, the higher we go, the flatter, more indefinite, more marshlike the terrain becomes. Then the sun sinks and everything is permanently black and silver.

We keep on through the night, though the muddy track bumps and winds. The sky is clear except for one huge cloud. The moon seems to get fuller as the night goes on. We drive and halt throughout the night, sleeping for an hour here, stopping for an hour there because we are stuck or because Sui has to present someone with a pair of shoes or a plastic flower – it must come as a shock to the recipient at 3 a.m. Snow lies on either side of the road. The moon goes behind the cloud. Shooting stars plummet to extinction, and a globular soft green glow falls gently to earth as we approach the ridge. Sui calls it *qinghaodan*: is this something like St Elmo's fire? We do not talk much. Each of us has his afflictions now: I have my headache, a sore arm from wielding gunny bags and a pain in my leg from the damp socks I have been wearing. Sui now has his smokers' cough compounded by a running eye. Gyanseng has neck- and toothache, and wishes even more fervently that he had got a flight from Germu.

> The truck: two ravens caw.
> Yaks stare with panicked eyes,
> Then scatter. Wide plains draw
> Rays down from wider skies.

97

From Heaven Lake

The daylight, rising higher,
Burns through thin air to grass;
At night globes of green fire
Float on the pastured pass.

Cold in the mudlogged truck
I watch the southern sky:
A shooting star brings luck;
A satellite swims by.
The Silver River flows
Eventless through the night.
The moon against the snows
Shines insular and bright.

Here we three, cooped, alone,
Tibetan, Indian, Han,
Against a common dawn
Catch what poor sleep we can,
And sleeping drag the same
Sparse air into our lungs,
And dreaming each of home
Sleeptalk in different tongues.

10

Northern Tibet

13th August   By dawn we have descended the Tangula Range. When we reach the foot, we halt the truck and sleep for an hour or so. What a sudden change this is from the barrenness of Qinghai. Mist in well-formed strands moves across rich green hills. Yaks feed everywhere. A bright river keeps us company. Six trucks with Tibetan drivers pass us going in the opposite direction. Tibetans, unlike Hans, usually travel in convoys for company and Tibetan tea. Still early in the morning, we drive into Anduo.

This small town, with its bridge, military encampment and yards full of oil barrels, is one of the larger urban centres in Tibet. Tibet's population is under two million. Apart from Lhasa and Shigatse, there are a number of towns of regional importance; Anduo and Naqu are two of these that lie on the road to Lhasa.'

The area we will pass through to get to the high 'Trans-Himalayan' range before Lhasa is one of the most temperate in northern Tibet. It is moist, and supports rich pasture, unlike the bleak empty land of Chang Tang in northeastern Tibet. Anduo itself has a bustling air about it. Yaks stream over the bridge and down the street. Two trucks honk aggressively for the right of way. Tibetan children, astute-eyed, smiling, in warm and filthy rags, stand by the truck while we enter a teashop for a celebratory cup of tea. Gyanseng is the most cheerful of us three now that he is in Tibet.

'This tea is terrible,' says Gyanseng. We have asked not for yak-butter tea, the standard Tibetan drink, but for black tea with sugar and milk, also unobtainable before Tibet.

'I think the milk is off,' I remark.

'Don't worry – our sweet tea is usually much better than this. When we get to Lhasa tonight we'll have some. I know a couple of places that are open till after midnight.'

'Can you get sweet tea all over Tibet?' I ask Gyanseng. 'I thought most people preferred yak-butter tea.'

'The older people do. Most of us young people like sweet tea, too. I think the habit of drinking sweet tea came from India. So, for that matter, did the habit of smoking *bidi*s.'

'Can you get *bidi*s in Lhasa?' I asked, surprised. (*Bidi*s are small Indian cigarettes, conical in shape, with tobacco rolled up in a green tobacco leaf, after the manner of cigars.)

'Not often,' says Gyanseng. 'A Nepalese merchant might bring a consignment across from time to time. But in the 1950s they were freely available.'

'And alcohol? Can you get that easily in Lhasa?'

Gyanseng looks at me in astonishment. 'Of course. *Chang* – or *qingke* wine – everybody drinks it. Go to the Norbulingka Park on Sunday and you'll find people sitting on the grass with food and wine, drinking and singing. On Sundays my friends and I go along with our families for a picnic. We eat, tell stories and return home drunk, dancing in a procession. We send the children on ahead.'

This is a side of Gyanseng I cannot easily imagine. But as we get closer to Lhasa – we do not, as it happens, arrive tonight – he grows livelier and livelier, and even more companionable.

'Shall I sing you a Tibetan song?' asks Gyanseng when we are back in the truck. He begins, in a high, rhythmic and reedy voice. It sounds profoundly melancholy. It sounds to me like a song of parting or unrequited love. 'What kind of song was that?' I ask when he has finished.

'A drinking song,' he says.

We stop at innumerable houses on the way to our next town, Naqu. Many of them contain portraits of Chairman Mao, often next to pictures of the Dalai Lama. Incense sticks burn in front of both of them. We are given yak-butter tea to drink – a greasy yellow concoction, neither sweet nor clear, resembling soup more than tea. I do not enjoy it, but

Gyanseng and Sui down several cups. Sui must know the entire roadside population between Anduo and Lhasa. He transacts business, haggles over prices, gulps down tea, and enters notes in his small pink notebook. His eye weeps copiously today.

The nights in the truck have had more of a physical effect on me than on the other two. I have added attacks of sneezing to my list of woes. But there is an exhilaration to being in Tibet, especially in this lush and beautiful area we are driving through, that predominates over all thought of discomfort. Thick turf is divided in places by stone walls reminiscent of those in Wales. Dandelions, daisies and a silky deep blue flower spread themselves in sheets over the ground. Playful but stupid young yaks gambol about, kicking their hind legs in the air before breaking out into a gallop. We halt by the broad grassy bank of a river, which, I discover from my map, is a source of the Salween. Outside the Chang Tang, which is an area of internal drainage, almost every stream on the Qinghai-Tibet plateau is a source of some important river: the Yangtse, Mekong, Brahmaputra and Indus all have their headwaters here.

Around me on the grass are lumps of dry yak dung and clusters of yellow flowers. In the late afternoon hail falls out of a sunny sky. We are now near Naqu, and the view is another one of those red and green contrasts that are so brilliant as to seem unnatural. Rainwater gathers in red puddles, the red drainage gullies parallel to the road are full; the road itself, a strip of red, lies on a baize of completely flat greenery. On the horizon stands a complex yet symmetrical peak, covered with snow. A few horses are being driven towards Naqu, probably for the annual fair and horse-races held there at this time of the year.

Naqu is a town of a few thousand inhabitants, with an agricultural machinery factory, a powdered milk factory, and the usual contingent of yaks and troops. We meet a soldier friend of Sui's who is stationed here, and lives in tiny shack-like quarters. Photographs of his family and popular movie stars mingle promiscuously with posters of famous literary characters. Newspapers are stuck on the ceiling, from which a light bulb dangles. Such classics as *The Journey to the West* and *The Story of the Stone* sit on shelves next to movie magazines. He is from Lanzhou and is unhappy that he cannot obtain noodles in Naqu. People brought up on noodles don't like to switch over to a staple rice diet, and *vice versa*: this is one of the major differences between northern and southern Chinese.

Sui has brought him a supply of noodles and fresh vegetables from Liuyuan; his friend is delighted. After dinner I shave – ah, luxury – for the first time in days. The others are examining a chicken that has frozen to death on the top of the truck. The meat is still good, they decide. After they have plucked the chicken, we go to find a place to sleep. The Transport Yard contains a motley assortment of people: drivers, peasants, officials, even a lama in his deep purple robe. While the Tibetan women we have met today have been wearing Tibetan skirts, blouses and jewellery, the men have been dressed mainly in Chinese jackets and trousers. However, the yakherds or those who drive the horses to Naqu have also retained their traditional dress. I photographed one bright-eyed old yakherd as he sat with his dogs on a hill near Anduo. He watched with trepidation my attempt to photograph one of his yaks pissing, but could not resist laughing when the animal charged me. He gave me some advice in high-pitched Tibetan. If only I knew some Tibetan how much more interesting this trip would be. As it is, I can only understand Tibet through the filter of those Tibetans who speak Chinese, almost all of whom are under forty. How their elders view the rapid and irreversible changes that have occurred since 1959 is something I have no way of comprehending.

14th August   Tomorrow is Indian Independence Day. Reading Naipaul makes for sad and serious thought. I think about what the two countries have done for their people in the course of the last thirty years. One overwhelming fact is that the Chinese have a better system of social care and of distribution than we do. Their aged do not starve. Their children are basically healthy. By and large, the people are well clothed, very occasionally in rags. Most children in the eastern provinces go to school for at least five years; this is in practice, not just (as in India) on paper. Tibet will take a long time to achieve the standard of living of other parts of China; however, in this comparatively prosperous part of Tibet I have not, for instance, seen signs of malnutrition.

China does not have as severe a problem with its urban population as India does, largely because people are kept out of the cities by means of both controlled ration-coupon distribution and force. As for the Chinese measures for reducing the general population growth rate – by persuasion, incentive and sometimes severe sanction – they seem to be fairly effective. I would not be surprised if China reached zero population growth by the first third of the next century, say fifty years from now. At that point, as long as the national product does not actually fall, the Chinese people will not have to worry about sinking into deeper poverty; whereas the possibility of absolute immiseration hangs like a sword above the Indian people. Yet our measures to control population have been almost totally ineffective (or, for a short time, so excessively coercive as to cause a backlash). The fact that we have elections every five years means that the government is afraid to undertake projects that are unpopular but beneficial in the long term. The Chinese government is not thus fettered.

Yet the same tightly controlled system that is such an advantage in this case, has caused great damage in other areas. The Chinese government, for all its quasi-democratic propaganda, is not answerable to the people. A government official has a power over others that is almost immune to attack. There are no courts for effective redress of even blatantly unjust decisions by Party or state officials. When I emerge battered and bleeding from some attempt to get even the simplest information or permission or explanation from some stonewalling government agency, my Chinese friends assure me that it is far worse for them: their jobs, income, housing, and their children's future are all under administrative control. How can they voice any protest?

Because of this anxiety, and because the printing presses are controlled by the government, people are not willing to voice their views in public. As for the Chinese underground press, it is far less active than the Russian. The problem is partly technological: *samizdat* needs only a Cyrillic typewriter, while a Chinese publication requires a font of thousands of characters. However, another major factor is the strong tradition in China of obedience to established authority.

As a result, the most fearsome, almost irresistible, waves of mania can sweep over the country. The Cultural Revolution is one example, in which not merely everything foreign but everything that spoke of the Chinese past was condemned, and, if possible, obliterated. Temple after temple, mosque and memorial hall and monastery, painting and screen and book and vase, artefact and artist; almost anyone or anything vulnerable or creative or non-conformist was damaged or smashed. Much of the brilliance and beauty of a great civilisation was in a few years destroyed by its ideology-infected children, the Red Guards. This is something that is not likely to happen in the democracy – however halting, hypocritical and hopeless – that is India.

A related problem that faces China is the general inhibition of creativity and innovation. This applies particularly to literature, where only politically 'correct' works see the light of publication. Music and the visual arts are also affected, but to a lesser extent. What worries the authorities more, however, is that this stagnancy has also affected production. Few people want to innovate or invent, when the punish-ment for being wrong is so disproportionate to the reward for being right. Ideology and patriotism can be a substitute for material rewards – and the Chinese are a far more patriotic people than the Indians – but, as economic planners tend to find out, this is true only to a limited extent. The decentralising reforms that are currently taking place in field and factory alike aim at encouraging production through incentives; it remains to be seen how effective these will be. Yet it is difficult to say which works better – the cumbersome slow-reacting Chinese economy or our economy in India, with its inefficiencies and inequalities, and its huge governmental octopus, whose sole purpose seems to be to stifle the initiative it claims to be encouraging, and whose one tentacle doesn't know what the other seven are doing.

I remember reading a question in an economics textbook: 'If you were to be born tomorrow, would you prefer to be born in China or India?' If I could be guaranteed the lucky place in the Indian sweepstakes that I at present occupy, there is no question as to what my answer would be; even if I were poorer than the average Chinese child, I would still prefer to be in India. But if I were born to the inhuman, dehumanising misery in which the poorest third of our people live, to the squalor and despair and debility that is their life, my answer would not be the same. Man does not, of course, live by bread alone, but with so little of it he can hardly be said to live at all.

I am often asked (and I fear that a new spate of such questions will be forthcoming from the moment I arrive in Delhi) about the relative success of our two large overpopulated countries in satisfying the most basic needs of their people. What is sometimes forgotten when making this comparison is that, except for the greater mineral wealth of China (a result of its far greater land area), all the *a priori* advantages lie on India's side. India's needs are fewer, and its agricultural production possibilities are greater. First, less clothing and heating are required for the average Indian than for the average Chinese: everyone in the north of China needs both a heavy overcoat and heating fuel in winter. Secondly, India has more arable land per capita, more sunshine for double and triple cropping, and a better potential for irrigation. Yet despite all this, the average Chinese is better clothed, better fed and better sheltered than the average Indian.

But the Indian achievement of the last thirty years has been in a different, more nebulous, and in a sense more difficult direction. The country has not fragmented: a whole generation of Indians has grown up accepting that an independent and united India is the normal state of affairs. In the first few years of a nation, that is already a great deal: one cannot expect a powerful patriotism. A country with more than a dozen languages, with no strong historical tradition of unity, faces problems that a culturally and linguistically cohesive China does not even have to consider.

A second institution, equally difficult to preserve for a poor country, is democracy. Here again, for all the corruption and abuse that the Indian political system displays, it is, after a fashion, both representative (unpopular governments have twice been thrown out) and widely accepted (again, it seems to be the norm for those born after Independence). This is quite remarkable. Dictatorships of the left or right are no less corrupt than democracies. (One has only to read the Chinese *People's Daily* to be convinced of this.) They are, besides, far more arbitrary in their dealings with any person or institution guilty of independent thought or action: a court with independent powers to interpret a functioning constitution, a press that can criticise the executive, elections in which the executive can be dismissed; all these are anathema to those who desire total executive control. This is not to say that because India possesses such institutions, independent thought and initiative are common there, but that the conditions for their emergence exist.

When I first went to China I was far more blindly enthusiastic about its achievements than I am now. I now see that China's achievements are solid but have serious drawbacks; and that is about all that can be said about India's, too.

We set off early in the morning, the road a hard but slippery mud. The tracks on the road indicate that other trucks have been slithering all over the place, but Sui keeps a firm yet light control on the wheel. Our fuel is running low, so we fill up on oil and diesel at the Naqu filling station. Sui tells me that the attendants at Anduo and Naqu are very honest and never cheat their customers. He mentions this as if it were unusual.

We stop – this is the first of many halts – to see a Tibetan family that Sui knows. The woman is of astonishing beauty. She and Sui haggle spiritedly over the price of shoes while the children make cross-eyes at me. Soon afterwards we are having a cup of Chinese Ovaltine in a cold tent at a road-repair camp. Some of Sui's jauntier friends are entertaining us with a description of how they were caught gambling by the authorities. (There is a regulation against playing cards for money.) The disciplinary committee of the camp made them forfeit their monthly bonus. 'But it's so boring here. What is there to do in this fucking place? There're only army camps and road-repair camps and Tibetans.'

After innumerable similar interruptions to the journey, Gyanseng finally gets his own back: in a small settlement, as we are about to cross a bridge, Gyanseng catches sight of a friend and tells Sui to stop. We are invited into the friend's tent, which he shares with two other Tibetans and three Hans. Sui, for once, is not pleased about the delay and sits tensely on a bunk glancing at his watch. 'We have to be in Lhasa by this evening,' he says to Gyanseng. 'Yes, yes,' replies Gyanseng, echoing

Sui's previous placatory comments, 'Just one minute, five minutes, ten minutes, all right?' Sui is outmanoeuvred, and sips his yak-butter tea meditatively.

'Let's have lunch here,' says Gyanseng, and we are each given a bowl of *sampa*, a kind of roasted flour ground from highland barley. Into this we pour a little tea, and eat it with our fingers. The Hans and Tibetans in this tent live together in a cooperative segregation: language, food and attitudes divide them. The Hans complain about the hardships of living in Tibet; it is true that they are deprived of many basic items and cultural stimuli that they are used to, but this does not go far enough to explain why the Hans so despise the culture of Tibetans and other minorities. This attitude is not confined to those who have only received a primary education: many of my Chinese acquaintances, and, alas, some of my friends also share it.

Black yaks, white sheep flow over the green. Men on horseback guide them, also carrying thin logs across the plain. But where do logs come from in this treeless land? By the side of the road near Naqu, a flayed yak's carcass, red and huge, is being hacked apart by men with knives. A good deal revolves around yaks in this economy: transport, milk, meat, fur, hoof, dung, bone, pelt, tail; everything is used. What a versatile machine this is that can convert grass into clothing and butter and fuel and tent-hide.

Lhasa is now just a hundred and fifty kilometres away. We should be there in about four hours, probably before nightfall. The map is encouraging – a plain, a mountain range (the Trans-Himalayan range) and then the Lhasa valley. Gyanseng is warbling away. My headache cannot touch my high spirits. As soon as I get to Lhasa, I will begin formalities for further travel. I know it may take a long time, and my Chinese documents expire in two weeks. This worries me, but there is nothing I can do to expedite things. And today – if only we arrive before sunset – I will see the Potala.

This train of thought is punctured by Sui slamming on the brakes. The truck comes to a halt. Gyanseng and I ask him what the matter is.

Sui is looking for something on the floor of the truck among the bags and boxes. 'Fish,' he says. 'It'll be dark in a few hours.'

It transpires that Sui's wife likes fish, and Sui is now near one of his favourite fishing spots. He gets a net out from amongst the luggage. 'Let's catch fish in that stream,' says Sui. Gyanseng and I are not taken by the idea, especially as it is raining.

'Come on, it'll only take half an hour.'

'Nonsense,' says Gyanseng, 'it won't take half an hour. The stream is swollen because of the rains – there won't be any fish. But it will take you two hours to realise this.'

'No, no, I've fished here before,' insists Sui. 'Come along now, Gyanseng. Give me a hand with the net.'

We walk over to the stream through the damp tussocks and yak dung, spread the net and wait in the rain.

Two hours later, we are back in the truck. Gyanseng and I are quiet; there is a gleam of anger in Sui's eye. He drives the truck at a tremendous speed. The sun is now out and a beautiful rainbow colours the sky. But Sui is darkly obsessed. Gone is the pain of his weeping eye, gone the recognition that it is less than two hours to sunset; all he can think about, as he speeds along the now smooth and metalled road, is how to entice a fish into his net.

'Could we stop here just for a minute?' I say. 'I'd like to take a picture of the truck and the rainbow together.' We stop the truck, and before we know it, Sui has rushed off, carrying his bag along a pebbly country road, towards a small bridge over a stream. He rushes back excitedly. Quick as a flash he leaps into the driver's seat. 'Fish. I'm sure there are fish there,' he mutters, more to himself than by way of explanation. 'Left my net behind in the truck – really stupid.' We drive full tilt along the pebbly road, which is raised above the soggy pasture around. Suddenly we aren't moving any more. A wheel has got stuck in the soft mud beneath the pebbles and can find no grip. We rev harder but the wheels merely churn around on the surface. Sui curses and tries to reverse. The back wheel slips off the road into the waterlogged soil and wet grass.

For a few minutes Sui sits and curses with great vehemence. He then gets out of the truck and starts to work with the spade on the mud near the back wheel. Gyanseng and I follow him. We work with our hands to get some of the pebbles away in order to make a ramp for the back wheel to drive up on. A villager appears, sits down, laughs and makes no attempt at assistance. When Sui asks him in Chinese for some help, he tells him to help himself. Every time Sui gets the truck moving, the wheels slither and slip in the slush. We hoist the truck up with the jack and try to clear the mud from under the wheels. By now a small crowd has come from the village across the bridge. They watch us work in silence.

Gyanseng and I go over to the bridge, which is covered with chips of stone. We gather a few of these rough chips to replace the smooth pebbles under the wheels, so that the tyre can get some purchase on the ground. But the strategy is not a success and it is getting dark. Then Gyanseng goes to the villagers and talks to them in Tibetan; they come over to help. A tractor appears from across the bridge and is enlisted. It pulls, we push, but this is not enough. Two more spades are brought to the site of operations by a friendly middle-aged Tibetan couple. When it gets dark they ask the three of us to come over and have something to eat at their place.

Sui curses himself and the truck and the stream which, the villagers say, contains no fish. He refuses to come along.

'You go,' he tells Gyanseng and me. 'Eat if you want. I'm going to continue working.'

'It's dark,' I say. 'There's no point going on. Come on, Lao Sui. I'm certainly going.'

'So am I,' says Gyanseng. 'We may as well accept that we're going to be stuck here overnight. Let's at least eat something.'

'Go along, then,' says Sui angrily. He gets a torch out of his bag, lights it and places it on the step of the truck. He reverts to his frenzy of digging.

'Well, we'll bring something back for you,' says Gyanseng.

The hospitable couple have been waiting for us by the bridge. We go over to their house, a very long room with low couches which can be used for either sitting or sleeping on. They give us yak-butter tea and *sampa*, and various savoury preparations made of flour. Then we have noodles and yak meat and capsicum, with chilli powder sprinkled on top. It is the best meal I've had since Germu. Since our hosts are yawning, I refuse the yak-milk yogurt. While we eat they talk about their posting for a number of years on the Indian border, which is where their seven-year-old son was born. His mother accompanies us to the gate, giving us some savouries for Sui.

Meanwhile, Sui has been working himself into a fury with the world. We ask him to eat something, but he refuses it. 'I've brought all this upon myself,' he mutters.

'Look, Sui,' I say, 'Have something to eat.'

'I'll get us out, I tell you,' he replies.

'What are you going to do?'

'I'll continue digging out the mud in front of the wheels.'

'It'll do no good. We've tried it before.'

Sui doesn't answer. Gyanseng and I get back into the truck and wrap ourselves up against the cold. But Sui keeps working on the road in a kind of stultified self-rage in which it becomes immaterial that it is raining or freezing or that we are trying to get some sleep. Every half hour, he gets back into the truck and puts it into gear, but it is an exercise in futility. At four in the morning, having pushed the wheels in deeper, he gives up. Finally we get some fitful sleep.

15th August   At ten in the morning the situation is just as hopeless as ever. Gyanseng suggests digging the pebbly road up to get the wheels level. But it has rained, and the field around is even more waterlogged than before. Even if we get all four wheels down to the level of the sunken back wheel, the truck will still be too heavy for the soil.

'I think we'd better get help from somewhere,' I suggest. 'Perhaps a couple of vehicles might be able to help where the tractor failed.' Actually I don't know if this will work either, but what we are doing at the moment has no chance at all. Sui continues digging.

'Can't you give me a hand?' he asks irritably.

I too am irritated. Lack of sleep, a continuous headache and a rising sense of frustration bubble over in an indignant outburst. 'Sure I could,' I say, 'if I thought it would do any good. But all we're doing is digging ourselves in deeper. It isn't as if I haven't been helping.' Then I pause to calm myself. 'Why don't we get some help?' I continue.

'Let me do this my way, will you?'

'How long do you think it will take, by this method?'

'How can I tell you that?' asks Sui.

'It could be days at this rate,' I say, desperately. 'I've got to get to Lhasa soon. If we haven't got some help by noon, I'll have to go on to Lhasa myself.'

'How on earth will you do that?'

'I'll cycle there if necessary. It's only a hundred kilometres.'

'And where will you get the bike from? And what will you do with the luggage. It isn't safe for you, either. If you . . .'

'I'll borrow it from someone here. And . . .'

'Don't be childish,' says Sui, raising his voice. 'It's a ridiculous idea. Can't you be patient?'

In fact I too can see how stupid the idea is. But this doesn't prevent my next outburst. 'And what do you think is a sensible idea?' I shout. 'Sitting here with you catching fish?'

'Did you have to bring that up?' says Sui indignantly.

'Look . . .' I begin, but stop in sudden dismay. I have, I realise, made a most gratuitously cruel remark. I didn't realise I felt so resentful about this mess. Sui doesn't speak, either. I am afraid I have irreparably damaged things. I try to tell myself that something got into me, but I am ashamed of myself even as I continue to smoulder at him.

I walk towards the bridge, hoping to regain some clarity. A mind clouded with rage is fearsome even to itself. I look at the fishless stream, and try to understand why I feel so much rancour. It was his paternalistic comments that were the final straw, I tell myself. But then, haven't I been nagging him all along about his smoking? It was his fixation that got us into this mess in the first place, I think. But even if I believe in the attribution of blame for our situation, is there any balance between his anger and irritability and my sarcastic and selfish explosion? Finally, if I am extenuating my actions by hauling in headaches and tiredness as excuses, can I imagine what it must be like for Sui, who is cold, hungry and utterly exhausted?

The more I think, the worse I feel. I go through a replay of his kindness and companionship during the trip. What rights do I have in this matter of the truck anyway? And then there are the basic questions: do I like Sui? And if so, why don't I make it up with him? I walk back to the truck in a miserable frame of mind.

A small party crosses the bridge and moves down the pebbled road towards us: a Tibetan woman and three young children. They bear butter-tea in a thermos flask, and a bag of *sampa*. They have been sent by the hospitable couple to ensure that we do not go hungry. They have brought bowls with them, and ask us to eat. The little girl wears a Mao badge. They smile shyly and warmly. Mao still enjoys cult status in Tibet, judging from all the pictures and badges I've seen. In some cases children wear both Mao badges as well as Dalai Lama lockets – no longer forbidden, though doubtless disapproved of by the authorities.

It is a delight to eat simple food in such green, clear, fresh surroundings. A couple of horses graze in the meadow around us. The friendly four smile as they leave. We can exchange only goodwill as they speak no Chinese. I offer them some raisins and biscuits, which they stuff into their pockets, and then with a wave or two they head back across the bridge.

Something gives in my obduracy, and I walk over to Sui.

'Lao Sui, I'm sorry for what happened just now.'

Sui nods silently, not looking up at me. He is sitting by the back wheel, apparently intent on working.

I suppose this doesn't sound like much of an apology. I try again.

'What I said, I didn't say intentionally. I regret it.'

Sui looks at me in a way that is both friendly and restrained. 'Let's just forget it. I also said many things.'

We do not say anything for a while. Gyanseng, who has reverted to his Trappist role during our altercation, begins to hum tunelessly.

Feeling bad about what I have to say next, I go on. 'If it looks like nothing is going to happen today, I will have to go on to Lhasa with my papers. Maybe I can hitch a ride on the main road. I could leave my luggage with you. We'll meet in Lhasa when you get there. If they don't allow me to go through Nepal, I will have to get to Hong Kong before my ticket expires.'

Sui looks at the truck and sighs. 'I really don't know when we'll get out of this place,' he says. 'You'd better take your luggage along. We'll look you up when we get to Lhasa. You'll be staying in the Number One Guest House where they put all the foreigners.'

I get all my odds and ends into my bags and say goodbye. We should meet in two or three days. I struggle back down the pebble road: blue clothes, blue cap, small orange backpack, one large black bag, two small black bags. It is noon.

II

Into Lhasa

There are few trucks on the road at this time of day. Most drivers are eating lunch, or taking their *xiuxi* (afternoon rest). I put my luggage down, take out my map, and write 'LHASA' in both English and Chinese on the back. I hold up this sign and look hopeful, but the few trucks that appear zoom past. Opposite me is another hitch-hiker, a striking and robust woman who does not seem in the least concerned when trucks pass her by. She asks me something in Tibetan; I reply, 'Lhasa,' and she nods. A tractor-trailer, crowded with passengers, comes down the road and stops. Apparently they are relatives of hers, for there is a surprise reunion scene, with much embracing and shouting.

She leaves. I sit down again, looking expectantly at the far bend in the road. After an hour of waiting, I see a truck putter into view from the distance. It is moving very slowly indeed. The driver's eyes meet mine. The truck stops. He leans out of the window. 'Is that all the luggage you have?' he asks. 'Yes,' I reply. 'Well, hop in,' he says. The truck begins to crawl again along the smooth metalled road.

The driver is Tibetan, judging by his features and accent; he is friendly but uncommunicative. We exchange cigarettes at intervals. The truck chugs along steadily, though at a snail's pace. It is stuck in first gear. For my part I am very glad at least to be moving forwards.

The truck moves on. It starts to drizzle. The snow-capped hills on either side of the broad valley disappear in mist. We cross a stream on a narrow bridge; it is dark red, swollen by the rains of the last few days. But the road is excellent now.

We have just crossed the stream when a woman runs across from the grassland, into the middle of the road. The truck stops, and she explains

– in Tibetan, though I get the gist of the affair from her agitated gestures – that a truck she's been travelling in has got bogged down in the grass and needs to be pulled out. My driver seems reluctant, but the woman, who is middle-aged, charming and desperate, persuades him to pull off the road onto the spongy pasture. We drive towards the marooned truck, and are almost there when we get stuck ourselves. The woman is vociferously apologetic. Her companions, who are working on dislodging the other truck, come over to ours. We use ropes, and chains, and little stones under the tyres, and push, and dig, but to no avail. Then it begins to rain, and in sheets, so that we are thoroughly soused.

I can see a repetition of last night's impasse. I help the twenty or so people who are assembled there though there appears to be little chance of extricating the truck; but after an hour or so I tell the driver I will have to go on to Lhasa by myself. He suggests I try to hitch a lift and leave my luggage here in the dry cabin of the truck until I have found one. I walk back to the road, feeling rather like a rat who has left two sinking ships. Trucks zip and slosh past; I sneeze and shiver. Finally, in desperation, I walk back to the stream and stand on the bridge. A truck comes to an angry halt. 'What do you mean by obstructing us like this?' yells the driver. I explain what has happened and why I need to get to Lhasa so urgently. The driver is then sympathetic. He points to the tarpaulin awning at the back of the truck.

Under the awning, sitting on long benches, are about twenty high school teachers from, of all places, Liaoning, in northeastern China. It turns out that individual provinces in China have 'adopted' individual areas in Tibet for developmental and educational work. Naqu, the town in which there is a powdered milk factory, has been allotted to Liaoning; Lhasa has been allotted to Shanghai; and so on.

These teachers, all of them men, have been in Naqu district for over a year now, and have one more year to go. They are on their way to Lhasa for a five day sightseeing holiday, and are in high spirits: their work, in which I am interested, is the last thing they wish to talk about. They ask me a flood of questions about India, England and the United States, education and politics and travel, jobs and incomes and expenditures. They have just read in the newspapers about the dowry system in India, and about the recent bride-killings. In China there is a bride-price, not a dowry. Though the newspapers inveigh against this, it is a fact of life for a boy in China and for his family. In some cases the parents of the girl make enormous and unreasonable demands on the boy for furniture, clothes, and all kinds of fancy apparatus – radio, TV, watches, a bicycle, a sewing machine. In one case a Nanjing University student stole a thousand yuan from an old couple in order to fulfil his girl-friend's demands, and, when caught, killed himself. In the area where I did my research (three villages in Jiangsu) one of the larger items of annual expenditure for any family with sons was building materials. These are bought year after year from the time the boy is about twelve years old, a few logs one year, some bricks sold cheaply by the local kiln the next, tiles, cement, iron bars for the windows and so on. It is almost impossible for a boy in this rural area to get married unless he has a place of his own to live in.

One of the teachers from Liaoning, an untiring young man of twenty-three, insists on speaking in English with me. This is something that happens *ad nauseam* on the Nanjing streets whenever foreigners are spotted. No place is safe, no privacy respected by the worst of these 'language rapists', who are only interested in you for your language. You may be sitting on the balcony of the Drum Tower, sipping tea, watching the sunset, red and smoky, over the roofs of the city; you may be buying onions in the crowded market and trying to prevent yourself and your purchases from being crushed by your fellow customers; you may be standing in a bus, or at a bus-stop or at a counter in the post office; nowhere are you safe from the machinations of the language-rapist. He will smile at you determinedly, and begin a conversation – 'Hello. Do you speak English? So do I. What country are you from?' The first few times this is attractive, but it quickly palls. It becomes increasingly apparent that he is not interested in you. You are merely a punch-bag for language practice.

It is difficult therefore to avoid an immediate sense of irritation, almost a reflex rudeness. But the circumstances that have encouraged this behaviour should in fact arouse sympathy: many people – students, workers, government servants – are anxious (and sometimes compelled) to learn English, but the opportunities for speaking English are almost non-existent. True, there are Chinese radio and Voice of America and BBC programmes that teach the language, but this is not practice in conversation. True, there are a growing number of English teachers in Chinese universities and other institutions, some of whom are shamefully overworked by their departments and their own sense of duty or enthusiasm. But only a miniscule proportion of language learners can get at them; and even they do not have much time left after the wearying hours of teaching and correction. Small wonder, then, that some students of English batten onto any foreigner they see in the streets.

The teacher from Liaoning, though, is an exception. He uses the language to communicate, and does not merely speak it like a mechanical learner; this is the more remarkable since he could not have spoken with a native speaker once during his last year in Naqu. He is particularly interested in the educational systems of different countries. But he does not get much of a chance to pursue the subject, as the conversation is snatched up by his companions, and seesaws irresolutely between Chinese and English.

Now and then we look out at the passing hills from the opening at the back. The rain has cleared up; as we climb into the Trans-Himalayan range just before Lhasa we enter a spectacular landscape of gorge and cliff and turbulent river. The whole valley, much narrower than before, is green with grass and *qingke*, the hardy highland barley of the region. There are even clumps of trees here and there; and in the distance shining glaciers. The extent of habitation slowly increases as the valley widens. When I next look out we are already in the broad valley of the Lhasa River – with fields of wheat and barley, tall trees, buildings of cement, and, from far away, the dominating vertical plane of the Potala palace, monolithic and of an immense grandeur, white and pale pink and red and gold.

In this late afternoon light it is so beautiful that I cannot speak at all. I get up and stare at it, holding onto one of the supports at the back of the truck, and looking forwards in the direction we are travelling. The hill on which it rests, and its own thick, slightly slanting walls, combine to give it a powerful sense of stability; and the white and gold add an almost unreal brilliance to the vast slab that is its structure.

When the teachers get off at the Ministry of Light Industry Guest House (which, by some curious twist of *lianxi* arrangements, is where they are to stay), I ask if there might be place for me as well. There is a hurried exchange among the *lingdao* of the guest house. 'Sorry,' I am told. 'You had better report to the Lhasa Foreign Affairs Office and see where they allocate you.' The driver of the truck, without being asked, offers to take me there. We stop outside a gate, and after being challenged by the porter, I am allowed to enter. The porter makes a phone call, then asks me to sit down on a stool in the driveway and drink a cup of yak-butter tea. It tastes wonderfully warm. My clothes have not dried out from the soaking they took when I tried to get my last lift. I watch the roses and goats in the garden while I wait for something to happen.

A man in his mid-twenties appears, walking hurriedly towards us from behind the official buildings. 'This is Mr Ho,' says the porter.

'Ah, good evening. No, please don't get up,' says Mr Ho in excellent English. He sits down on a stool facing me and quickly gets down to business. 'What can I do for you?'

Mr Ho is Han, and of medium height. He has a sharp voice, fine, almost delicate features, and an observant manner that would make me more nervous than I already am if he didn't appear to be friendly as well. His wife and young son have followed him out. She stands knitting a sweater for the baby, who is running around the gravel-covered driveway pulling the hair of the porter's granddaughter.

'I don't really know,' I say. 'I was told by the *lingdao* at the Ministry of Light Industry Guest House to speak to someone from this office.'

Mr Ho looks perplexed. 'What were you doing there?' he asks. 'How did you manage to get a bus from the airport? Which group are you with?'

I decide to break the news gently. 'Actually, I'm not with any group. I'm travelling alone.'

'But this is quite irregular,' says Mr Ho. 'Which flight did you come in by? How many days have you been in Lhasa? Have you been staying at the Ministry of Light Industry Guest House?'

'Well, no,' I say blandly. 'I've just got to Lhasa. I hitch-hiked in. I'm afraid that's why I look so scruffy.'

'You *what?*'

'Look so scruffy.'

'No, no, I mean how did you get here?'

'I got a lift from Liuyuan on a truck. It was cheaper than flying. But it was all quite regular,' I say, anticipating him. 'Would you like to look at my travel pass? My student pass? I'm at Nanjing University . . .'

'Do the police know you're here?'

'No. I've just arrived.'

Mr Ho is alarmed. He looks at my travel pass. 'I must keep this,' he mutters. 'And your passport?' I hand it over.

'And why are you in Lhasa?'

'I'm on my way home. Through Nepal,' I say matter-of-factly.

If Mr Ho was alarmed before, now he is profoundly agitated. 'No,' he says. 'No, no – it's impossible. You will have to go back. By air. Which flight should I book you on? To Xian or to Chengdu? You must first go to Nanjing. Then you can find your way back to India. There are planes from Hong Kong, I'm sure.'

I have been expecting this. 'I don't have the money,' I say. 'The plane fare for foreigners is twice that for Chinese.'

'Yes. That's a regulation. It can't be waived.' Mr Ho pauses. 'If you don't have money, how are you going to stay in Lhasa?'

'Oh, I could pay the regular six yuan a night that students are charged.'

'No, no,' says Mr Ho, getting more and more upset, and speaking now in Chinese. 'That may be the practice in the rest of China, but Tibet is different. It costs everyone two hundred and fifty yuan a day to stay here.'

'What? Two hundred and fifty?'

'Yes. There's the foreigners' guest house and the guided tours and the translator and the jeep . . .'

'Well, I don't want any of that. I'd be spending several times more in one day here than during the whole journey from Liuyuan. I'll be my own translator and guide and I'll get a bus and live in a Chinese guest house. How was I to know that prices in Tibet would be different from the rest of China?'

'No, you have to stay in the Number One Guest House, where foreigners stay. And I'll book you on tomorrow's flight out of Lhasa.' He tries to look firm, but his sensitive face rebels.

'How can I pay for that flight when I can't even pay for the hotel?' I plead.

'Borrow some from another foreign student. Phone Nanjing University,' suggests Mr Ho in desperation.

'The university won't pay for my travels; I'm not on a project,' I reply. 'And my foreign friends are travelling all over China – it's their summer holidays – and I don't know where they are. Besides, they're probably hard up too.'

We sit for a few minutes, not saying anything. It is now dark but the goats are still grazing in the garden. I feel sympathetic towards Mr Ho, who has been disturbed at home on a Saturday evening by an impoverished and importunate *waibin* with no place to stay, nowhere to go and who hasn't even reported to the police yet.

I break the silence. 'It'll be cheapest for me to go back via Nepal,' I say. 'I have a valid exit visa with no specified port of exit.'

'Yes,' says Mr Ho, now much calmer. 'I saw your exit visa when I was examining your passport. But it doesn't apply to Tibet. Tibet is different.'

'In what way?' I ask. This is serious. I had assumed that there would be some time-consuming paperwork in Lhasa, but had hoped that no new and essential document would be required.

'You need specific exit permission for Tibet. It's a land border.'

'So is Hong Kong, if you leave by train,' I point out with excited pedantry.

'Look, Mr Seth, it's not me who made the regulations,' says Mr Ho. He continues in a not unkindly manner. 'But even if you had this specific permission, not to mention an entry visa to Nepal, which I notice from your passport you don't . . .'

'Indians don't require a visa for Nepal,' I interrupt.

'. . . Yes? Well, even if all your documents were in order, you couldn't get to Nepal from here.'

I stare at him uncomprehendingly.

'You see, the Lhasa-Kathmandu road has been destroyed by floods and the Friendship Bridge on the border has been washed away. This happened last month. You are a little too late.'

I hold my head in my hands. I had expected a certain amount of bureaucratic obstruction, but not a natural disaster. The bridge must have been down even before I began my journey back in Beijing, and I never heard about it. No-one in the Nepalese Embassy mentioned anything when I said I planned to return through Lhasa.

I am about to ask about the possibility of repairs when Mr Ho goes on, quietly. 'It will take months to repair those sections of the road that have been washed away. As for the Friendship Bridge over the Bhotakoshi, that will probably take years to reconstruct, especially since all kinds of agreements will have to be signed between the two governments before work can begin. You might want to confirm this with the Nepalese Consul-General in Lhasa. Please believe me. Staying in Lhasa and waiting will do no good.'

I don't say anything. I can hardly believe I am so close to Nepal and yet will have to go thousands of miles in a huge loop to get home by a different route. I have got to think of something else. There has got to be something else I can do.

Mr Ho puts a consoling hand on my shoulder. 'As for tonight,' he says, 'I'll see what I can do to arrange a room at a reasonable rate. Maybe you'll be able to stay in Lhasa for two or three days and have a chance to look around before leaving for Nanjing. I'm very sorry about all this.' He goes to make a few phone calls, and returns with a pleased expression on his face. I am to stay at the Number One Guest House, according to the *guiding*, but will be charged at the Chinese, not the foreigners' rate. It will cost me ten yuan a night. The manager grumbles a bit when we get to the guest house, but accepts that it's a 'special circumstance'. I lie down exhausted on my bed, and slowly empty my mind of all future plans: if I want to think about Nepal I will have to do so when calmer. The dark outside is soothing. I have been put in an empty double bedroom. I borrow the second quilt to keep myself warm, and eat a few raisins I have soaked in hot water. By the time I have got through these mechanical motions, I feel refreshed and relaxed enough to take a short stroll outside.

It is now late, and my first impression of Lhasa is not a particularly visual one. Dogs bark continually; mangy beasts, both loved and uncared for, they roam around the streets fighting with each other and yapping at the occasional truck that roars down People's Road. As elsewhere in China, part of the attraction of sitting behind the wheel is the joy of being able to blow the horn, and even at night this capability is exercised to the full. Groups of pilgrims wander down the road in the direction of the old town, chanting and singing. I follow them for a while. The smell of urine and yak-butter and burning aromatic herbs infuses the air. In the gently lit square near the great Jorkhan temple, the pilgrims drink and dance in a ring, arms linked, men and women singing alternately. Others walk clockwise around the Jorkhan, talking in quiet voices until late at night.

I return to the guest house but cannot sleep. It is Independence Day, and the end of my journey to Lhasa. Even if I cannot go on from here, I should be thankful. A dream, rather, an obsession, has been fulfilled; and tomorrow I will begin looking around the town. If, at the worst, I have to make the circuitous journey back home via Hong Kong, it will still have been very well worth while.

12

Lhasa

The only foreign mission in Lhasa is the Nepalese Consulate-General, which lies among trees and fields at the western end of town. It is guarded by a sentry box. Since it is so rarely visited, the sentry is often not in, but is to be found instead strolling, rifle in hand, around the lane beyond the Consulate, with a gait that speaks of unutterable boredom. When I arrive at the gate, he sees me and comes panting back, in time to detain me with fifteen minutes of interrogation. Finally he makes a phone call. I look at the sign above the gate, which reads *Mahavanijya Dootavas* in the Devanagari alphabet. It is vaguely comforting to see the familiar script. The gate opens and a man wearing the conical hat of the Nepalis asks me to enter. Mr Shah, the *Mahavanijyadoot* himself, will be with me shortly.

I sit in the long hall and wait. Pictures of the King and Queen of Nepal stare unnervingly down at me across the low tables and ashtrays and carpets. It is ironic that my first morning in Lhasa should be occupied with planning how best to move on. The Consul-General, Mr Shah, soon appears. He is a striking man: gold teeth, wild black hair and flashing eyes. After a few preliminaries, I say I would like to ask him for his advice on a matter of travel.

'Yes?' he asks, expectantly.

'I've been told that the road and bridge between Tibet and Nepal have been swept away by floods. I didn't hear about this when I was in Beijing. I thought I'd ask you when this happened, and when you think it might be repaired.'

'How did you come to hear of this?'

'Mr Ho, down at the Foreign Affairs Office, mentioned it to me.'

'Well, it's quite true.' Mr Shah pauses. 'They're working on the road on both sides of the border. On the Nepalese side it's motorable until Lamasangu. On the Chinese side it's motorable until Nilamu. I don't know whether in the last few days they've been able to get any further, but I doubt it. It's been raining heavily.' He offers me a cigarette, a Zhonghua, one of China's best brands.

'Have you ever travelled by this road?' I ask.

'Yes, when I came here from Kathmandu about six months ago to take up this post. It's a two-day journey, and the road is good, or, rather, it was. The bridge over the Bhotakoshi at Zhangmu will take a long time to repair: maybe more than a year.'

So much, I think, for that route. I go on, a little doubtfully. 'There are no flights between Lhasa and Kathmandu, I suppose?'

'No,' laughs Mr Shah. 'No flights at all.'

'Not even private planes, for instance, for consular officials to get back to Nepal?'

'No. In fact when I return I will have to fly to Chengdu, then change planes for Kunming, get another plane for Rangoon, another for Calcutta, and a final flight to Kathmandu.' He smiles at the thought. 'I wouldn't advise it,' he continues. 'It takes a week.'

But the alternative is an even longer loop, via Nanjing and Hong Kong. 'I don't know,' I comment. 'Rangoon sounds attractive.'

It is clear that Mr Shah is not taken by Rangoon, but he encourages me nevertheless. 'Yes, well, I hope you enjoy it.' He puffs at his cigarette, going over a few details in his mind. 'You have a Burmese visa?'

'No,' I say uneasily.

'You can only get that in Beijing. You could send your passport in, but that could take weeks.'

Another possibility gone, I think. I may as well give up. Mr Ho was right. I have no choice but to return via Nanjing and Hong Kong. 'So I suppose that's that,' I say. My headache, fitful over the last day, is returning with psychosomatic vengeance.

But Mr Shah muses on. 'Well, when the floods occurred, there *were* some Nepalese citizens trapped on the Chinese side of the border. We asked the Chinese authorities for permission to land a helicopter to evacuate them, but this was refused. Somehow or other, though, and I don't know quite how, they crossed the river and have made it back to Nepal.'

'Yes?' I say, with a small surge of hope.

'Let me draw you a map of what I think they must have done,' says Mr Shah. He draws a north-south line for the Bhotakoshi river, and a few tributaries on both banks. 'The border is somewhat complicated in this area,' he remarks. 'Here, you see, it is marked by the Bhotakoshi itself, but here and here by the tributaries of the river. So there is a northern section where both banks of the Bhotakoshi are in China, a middle section where one is in China, and a southern section where both are in Nepal. The Friendship Bridge at Zhangmu used to be in the middle section, so that when you crossed the bridge you crossed the border at the same time. Do you follow me?'

'Yes,' I say, my eyes on the map.

'Now, after the river rose and swept away the bridge, there is only one way that the Nepalese trapped on this side of the river could have got across.' Mr Shah pauses professorially. His wild hair gives him an almost Einsteinian appearance. 'They must have walked southwards until they found a bridge on the Bhotakoshi which was still intact. Once they crossed the river they could go on to Kathmandu or wherever they wished.' He marks out the route with his finger, which I follow like a mesmerised pigeon.

'Have you thought of *walking* across the border?'

'No.' I am becoming increasingly inarticulate in the face of this possibility. Mr Shah has a pleasant voice.

'As I said, the road on the Chinese side is good until Nilamu. From Nilamu to Zhangmu and from there to Lamasangu you'll have to walk – perhaps three or four days on foot, depending on the weather and the state of the forest tracks. If there were a road a truck could do all this in a couple of hours. But it's possible on foot, as long as you get a good guide through the hills. And once you've got to Lamasangu you can take a bus to Kathmandu, and then a flight to Delhi: you might want to think about this.'

I might.

The Consul-General puffs at his cigarette in silence for a minute. 'There is only one problem,' he remarks.

'Oh?'

'Your visa.'

'But I thought I didn't need one for Nepal,' I say, in surprise. 'The Nepalese Embassy in Beijing told me that Indian citizens . . .'

'No, you don't need one, and even if you did I could issue you one here.' Mr Shah looks grave. 'I mean the Chinese exit visa. I don't know if they'll give you special permission to exit through Tibet.'

'How did the Nepalese get permission?'

'They don't need it if they live within a thirty kilometre zone along the border. There's an agreement to that effect.'

'Ah.' I don't know what to say.

'Sometimes they give permission, sometimes they refuse it. When my predecessor was here, two women, an Australian and a Swede, I think, got a lift in his jeep to Kathmandu. But with the bridge down, the Chinese authorities have become much more sticky. Two *National Geographic* photographers who flew into Lhasa last month were refused permission to cross into Nepal even though I'd given them Nepalese visas. I don't know what reason was given to them. All I can do is wish you better luck.'

I walk over to the Norbulingka Park, deep in thought, but with my headache miraculously cured. The sun is shining, the air is crisp, the sky is blue, and there are ancient trees all around. It is Sunday afternoon, and, just as Gyanseng described it, the park is full of people. To protect themselves from both sun and the sudden afternoon showers, families have stretched large sheets of coloured cloth from tree to tree. They sit on the grass and talk, or watch the scruffy deer in the small zoo, or stroll across to see the Tibetan opera being performed in the open air. The crowd leans forward as a woman kneels and a man reads out a long proclamation. Two warriors fight with stylised bloodthirstiness. Recitative is followed by song and dance. In the various forms of Chinese opera, some of the accompanying instruments are melodic; here, however, there are just drums and gongs. Nearby, two children, unconcerned by the spectacle and noise, are busy stirring a puddle with a stick. I take a photograph of them, and am just about to take another when I hear a voice behind me, in English.

'Hello! Which country are you from?'

'Please don't disturb me,' I say sharply. 'I'm taking photographs.' But it is too late: the children have moved off. Repenting of my rudeness, I turn to speak to the man. He is tall, about twenty-five, dressed in the standard Chinese jacket and baggy trousers, but from his darker skin and sharper features I guess that he is Tibetan. He has friendly eyes, and does not seem to have been offended by my brusqueness. He is nibbling at what looks like a very doughy biscuit.

'India,' I say. 'You are Tibetan?'

'Yes. I am Tibetan.' He speaks carefully, so as not to trip himself up over a grammatical obstacle. 'You have come to Lhasa for what reason?'

'I have come to Lhasa on my way home. I am a student. And you?'

'I live in Lhasa.'

'I mean, what work do you do?'

'I work here in a factory. I learn English in the evenings. Learning English is hard.'

'I think you speak well,' I say mildly.

There is a pause, and I do not know how to go on. These purposeful exchanges in English are all so similar, I think. I look at the biscuit in his hand and realise that I haven't eaten anything since last night's raisins. 'Where can I buy some biscuits?' I ask. 'Is there a shop nearby?'

'Come with me, please. You will meet my family.' With a pleasant mixture of formality and assertiveness Norbu ignores my splutterings and leads me to where about twenty people – more a clan than a family – are sitting on the ground below a cloth canopy: aunts, uncles, cousins, nephews, nieces. Their voices rise and fall in a joyful babble. His father is gambling with friends in a corner. Children are yelling above the hubbub. Norbu introduces his girlfriend, who is very shy. She offers me a bowl of yak-butter tea.

The only common language for the three of us is Chinese, and Norbu speaks it beautifully, despite the fact that he has never been outside Tibet. His father, who was in India many years ago, interrupts his game

for a few minutes to talk about Darjeeling in the 1930s, the music of
Sahgal, and, when I ask him a direct question, about changes in Tibet –
though in terms of cautious generality. He, like his son, is a tall and
well-built man, but there is a curious frailness to him,

> 'As if some dire constraint of pain, or rage
> Of sickness felt by him in times long past
> A more than human weight upon his frame had cast.'

But gossiping and gambling with his friends, he seems happy enough.
He drinks *chang* (*qingke* wine) from a silver bowl, and I am given a bowl
too. It tastes like a dry white wine, enjoyably though not overpoweringly
potent. Huge tins of sweet and savoury biscuits and home-made snacks
are passed around, and everyone in turn is made to sing a song (I dust off
the perennial favourite, 'Awara'). Even the shyest little girl sings with
great gusto. When I leave I am filled with their contagious happiness. It
is some days later before I become aware of the harsh backdrop against
which this lighthearted scene has been played.

Bath hour is not yet over in the Number One Guest House; a steaming
hot shower rids me of the dust and dirt of the journey. The soapy water
pours off my hair in a black stream, and the warmth feels exquisite to my
fatigued and neglected body. Downstairs, I meet a group of Italians who
are here on a 'Tibet Safari'. They are quite young as far as tour groups
go – about fortyish – and very lively, though unfortunately constrained
by the programme organised by their Tourist Office guides. We drink
lemon and orange juice which they have prepared from packets of
powder. I am intoxicated by the sound of their names – Addilio, Ettore,
Gigi, Emilio, Marina, Igea . . .

Ettore and I, who can communicate only through gestures and pidgin
German, go to the Jorkhan temple the next day. This temple, located in
the centre of the old town, in the middle of an octagonal circuit of
streets, is one of the holiest centres of Tibetan Buddhism, and, with its
gold roof sloping elegantly above the busy street, one of the most
beautiful. The buildings around it are typically Tibetan, of white stone:
there are shops and dwellings on the first floor, deep narrow cells whose

interiors can only be dimly glimpsed. At the temple itself we are stopped by a 'responsible person' and spend three-quarters of an hour trying to get in, persuading and protesting by turns. Three ultra-bureaucratic and mendacious unit-leaders – for this temple, too, is a 'unit' – haul us to the office and growl aggressively on, Cerberus-like, about regulations and foreigners and introductory letters. (When I go to the Potala I will make sure I shed all signs of foreignness.) When I counter one argument, they switch to another: there are no monks 'on duty', the keys are not available. Eventually I get through to Mr Ho on the phone, and he solves the problem, suggesting at the same time that I be calmer in my approach to things. Upon payment of 10 yuan we are allowed to go in. (For 150 yuan people are permitted to take photographs in the rooms).

We see the magnificent inner hall of the temple, with niches and alcoves in the sides, silk hangings, fragrant yak-butter lamps. Murals in reds and greens give life to the walls, and within the halls are gold Buddhas, each with a different expression or posture or gesture; future and past Buddhas, Guanyins and Sakyamunis; Buddhas compassionate and Buddhas calm. The most important Sakyamuni is protected behind a heavy chain-meshed entrance.

The Jorkhan Temple (I learn from the introduction to a set of postcards) was first built by the Tibetan king Songtsan Gambo in the middle of the seventh century, and has been damaged and repaired several times through the centuries. In 1961 the temple was listed by the State Council of the People's Republic as an ancient monument selected for special protection, but it nevertheless suffered heavy damage during the Cultural Revolution. It has been restored since then. What a tragedy that such beauty should still be so unpleasantly inaccessible.

King Songstan Gambo (who is also said to have founded the Potala) is credited with introducing Buddhism into Tibet, having reputedly been converted by his Chinese and Nepalese wives, both Buddhists. While the monarchy died out a few generations later, Buddhism went on growing and gradually replaced Bön, the former shamanistic religion of the area. By the eleventh century it appears that secular power was also in the hands of a number of Buddhist communities.

Many of the earliest Indian gurus who came to preach in Tibet were greatly influenced by Tantric Hinduism; some of the first classics to be translated into Tibetan were consequently Tantric texts. This undercurrent of Tantrism, together with survivals from Bön shamanism, give the Buddhism of Tibet much of its unique flavour.

One figure, the great Tsongkapa (died 1419) stands out in the history of Tibetan Buddhism. He reformed and consolidated the practice of the religion so comprehensively that there is hardly an institution that does not bear his imprint. The 'yellow hat' or 'reformed' sect (which became the established sect in Tibet); the three monasteries near Lhasa – Gandian, Drepung and Sera; the system of rule and ritual for monks and initiates; all these were founded during his life under his direction, or else soon after his death. In addition to this he was a renowned teacher of esoteric Buddhism, which is communicated not through texts but directly from teacher to disciple.

The spiritual leadership passed on after Tsongkapa to a series of high lamas. Later, with the help of the Mongolian princes (Mongolia had meanwhile been converted to Buddhism), secular power was concentrated in the hands of the Dalai Lama, whose seat was Lhasa. The Panchen Lama, whose seat was the Zashilumpo monastery in Shigatse, had no secular power but a spiritual position second only to the Dalai Lama. In time the high lamas themselves began to be worshipped, both in life and after death; a complex pantheon of Buddhas, Bodhisattvas and Lamas can be seen in all the great temples and monasteries of Tibetan Buddhism even today.

In the outer court of the Jorkhan, facing the street, worshippers are grinding flour, spinning prayer-wheels, chanting incantations. The air is filled with the scent of herbs and dust. Two men are circling the temple, prostrating themselves, marking with a stone the spot that their heads touch, rising, moving to the spot marked, and then prostrating themselves again. Like spinning the prayer-wheel, this is a way of accumulating merit. For some reason the crowd of people gathered around them cheers one and jeers the other.

Opposite the Jorkhan stands a withered tree, more than a thousand years old, brought by a Tang princess from China when she married King Songtsan Gambo; pilgrims from all over Tibet are camped below it in yak-hide tents, together with a number of smiling and grubby children with matted hair. I move around the octagonal street clockwise like everyone else (except the army jeeps and a sample of variously-sized belligerent dogs). I am followed by a troop of leech-like hawkers selling pieces of jade, turquoise earrings, daggers, old Tibetan religious objects and ornaments and silver coins. Women sell yak yogurt in plump glass jars at corners; also joints of yak meat, pieces of yak bone, tomatoes, spring onions and a dark hard cheese-like substance that I buy, to my almost immediate regret. A crisp cucumber helps me to forget the strange taste.

The Han population of Lhasa is now greater than the Tibetan population, but this part of the old town is almost exclusively Tibetan. Even here, near the Jorkhan, the blue jackets and trousers are common, but it is the varied clothing of the Tibetans that catches the eye. The tall pilgrims from Chamdo are the most striking: red string intertwined with their hair, daggers hanging from their belts, they have a fierceness of facial expression well-suited to their martial bearing. A woman from Qinghai has her hair plaited in a complex ornamental panel behind her, which reaches almost to her waist, and three strips of banded cloth fall like an apron in front of her dress. She emerges from a tent, pulling a wailing child behind her. Four small boys catch sight of my camera; their faces caked in grime and snot, healthy in their ragged clothes, they run after me begging for money. An old woman sits behind a wooden table covered with brightly striped cotton, cutting off prayer-flags from a long bolt of cloth. She is also selling silver ornaments, religious objects, plastic combs, hair curlers, small locks, cloth shoes, yak leather boots, inner soles, lacquer cups, postcards, two or three books and a large frayed orange carpet with a dragon design. A man wearing a green felt bowler hat lures me into the back of a shop and attempts to sell me a dagger. I am not interested. Its scabbard is encrusted with semiprecious stones. I am still not interested. Am I interested in a thirty centimetres high Buddha statuette? It is, he tells me repeatedly, very beautiful. It comes from a temple, but the man is unwilling to say how he came by it.

No, I am not interested. Will I at least look at it? No. It is only on the sixth refusal that he releases my arm.

My arm is next grabbed by a couple carrying a silver prayer-wheel. Murmuring '*kuchi-kuchi-kuchi*', they point at my camera. I try to show them that this is not a Polaroid, but they are adamant. When I snap a couple of shots, they demand money. I refuse; they move away without, surprisingly, any sign of ill-will. As I walk away from the octagon in the direction of the guest house, the green bowler makes yet another venal overture. I tell him to leave me alone. To buy such things as his beautiful Buddha is to encourage further plunder of the temples and to help degrade objects of reverence to assessable and saleable pieces of loot.

The sun is strong by ten in the morning, when I walk over to Mr Ho's office to tell him I'm thinking of walking to Nepal. Mr Ho is flustered. His baby son is playing outside, picking up handfuls of gravel and gurgling. He offers his son a boiled sweet to distract him – Chinese parents often resort to boiled sweets – and tells me that the police want to interview me. When would be best? Tomorrow morning? The sooner the better, I say. I ask him to mention my plans so that they can at the same time ask me whatever questions they want to about my onward journey. Time is running out. The few days left on my travel pass and residence permit are one by one trickling away.

In a department store, distressingly similar to those in other cities of China (except, perhaps, that AA batteries are even less available here), my eye falls on a toy bear with a camera. The bear moves: its head nods, it lifts its camera to eye-level, and a light flashes. On impulse I buy the bizarre beast for Mr Ho's little boy. But as I leave the store I begin to wonder whether I should have bought it. If I give it to Mr Ho now he may consider it an improper gift as my case is under consideration. If I give it to him after I have got my special exit endorsement, it may be seen as a reward, again improper. It occurs to me that the only appropriate circumstance in which I can give it is if I don't get permission to exit through Tibet.

With this depressing speculation in mind, I enter the guest house to hear that the Public Security Bureau has sent some people around. I am first examined in a general way by an officer called Zhao, clad in the immaculately clean and pressed white jacket and trousers of the police. Her questions, it seems to me, are intended as a check of my bona fides. In a fog of relevant and irrelevant details, she presses me again and again on crucial points – my status, my purpose in coming to Tibet – asking me, in a comprehensive but circumlocutory way, to explain everything that could be construed as an inconsistency. Five minutes after she has left, two other officers enter, a Long and a Liu. They have with them the sheet of paper on which Zhao took notes. At first they go over the same ground. I pull out letters and testimonials and certificates and research forms, anything that is printed or might look official, again regardless of relevance. When they ask about my proposed route to Nepal, I bring out the map that Mr Shah has drawn. I also enquire about the possibility of going directly to India via the road through Yadong. This idea is immediately rejected.

The officers are totally non-committal about whether or not I will get permission to exit from Tibet. The matter has to be decided 'in consultation', but with whom I cannot discover. I mention that unless I am out of Lhasa when my Chinese residence permit expires at the end of the month, it will be their duty to arrest me. They laugh politely.

By this time Mr Shah (who has invited me for dinner) has arrived at the guest house to give me a lift. He sits in a long black car with a long black cigarette holder in his mouth. The officers peep out of the window and are suddenly apologetic. They suggest that we continue the interrogation later; but I want to get it over with once and for all. When, ten minutes later, they leave, they take with them my passport and travel pass: I feel a little naked without them. I ask the police when I should contact them again; they tell me that they will get in touch with me. I ask them when that might be. 'When we have come to a decision,' they reply. 'Things take time.'

At the Consulate-General, over Haig on and off the rocks and *lassi* (made from yak yogurt – the first *lassi* I've had in years), Mr Shah and I reminisce about Patna. I lived there for ten long years. Mr Shah was there for only two – he studied international relations at the university – but he feels a greater attachment to Patna than to Delhi, where he has

worked for much longer. 'Ah,' he says, dandling his daughter on his lap, 'when I flew over Patna the last time, I pointed out the Golghar granary to my wife – and the red-bricked Darbhanga House, where I lived as a student; I made lifelong friends there, and got addicted to Charminar cigarettes. In 1955 they used to cost two annas for a pack of ten.' We do not speak in English today, and when Mr Shah says he is surprised that I haven't lost all my Hindi after living abroad for so many years, I am absurdly pleased. When he offers to send information about my safe arrival in Lhasa to my family (by radio relay), I am ecstatic. My message –
'DEAR MAMA PAPA SHANTUM AND ARADHANA I HAVE ARRIVED IN LHASA AND WILL BE IN KATHMANDU IN A FEW DAYS DO NOT WORRY ABOUT ME LOTS OF LOVE VIKRAM' – is perhaps over-optimistic, but I have downed a good deal of Mr Shah's Scotch by this time.

Next morning I walk across People's Street to buy a map of Lhasa at the bookstore. Inside, between 'literature' and 'technology', is an altar to Mao: a white bust of the Great Helmsman, surrounded by a low semi-circular wall of his maroon-bound books, with flower vases at each end. Huge red quotations from his works hang on the walls. As I stare at this shrine (the remnant of a past age; one no longer sees such monstrosities in the rest of China), I feel a sudden weakness in my legs, and almost collapse, so that I have to support myself against a counter. The shop assistants are alarmed at what must look like an overpowering spiritual revelation. They offer to escort me back to the guest house. I am all right, I insist. The guest house is just across the street.

But I am not all right. I have barely got back to my room when I collapse on the bed. All the old symptoms of headache, nausea and shortness of breath are back, together with an attack of diarrhoea for good measure. I have over-exerted myself, and have drunk too much alcohol; both unwise at this altitude. I order myself to spend a day in bed, and to suppress all exploratory instincts.

I spend the day writing postcards: this seems a surreal activity in Lhasa, but then the guest house attendants are playing frisbee outside my window and whistling 'Santa Lucia'. I look over a book I bought in Dunhuang: *Everyday Language for Hotel Personnel – 1000 English Sen-*

tences. Tourism is now a big thing in China: new five-star hotels are going up in several cities, under collaboration contracts with foreign firms. The book includes sentences like 'I want to have a manicure,' and 'Please curl the hair on the temples towards the front, curl the hair on the sides outwards, and make the hair on top higher.' 'There are some cockroaches in this room; please clear them out immediately.' 'It is a misunderstanding, I am afraid. The Chinese people and the Japanese people are very friendly towards each other.' On that cheerful note I close that book and open my *Lao Tzu*.

13

The Potala; Drepung; Norbulingka; a house in the old town

By Wednesday I feel energetic enough to get out of bed. The Potala, once the winter palace of the Dalai Lama – part fortress, part prison, part holy shrine of Lamaism – is a few minutes' walk from the guest house. It rises sheer and vast from the hill on which it rests. By the time I have climbed to the public entrance I am dizzy again. I pay thirty cents and am propelled forward into the building by the huge crowd – and from then until I am squeezed out at the exit, I have little control over my movements. The mass of people, pilgrims from everywhere in Tibet, devout and curious, chanting, praying, shoving against each other, spinning prayer-wheels, giving offerings to the Buddhas, and ladling yak butter from jars into the lamps, has reached a pitch of religious enthusiasm that is, to my exhausted senses, both exalting and disturbing. Impression blurs with impression, and later I cannot remember what any particular room was like. Everywhere there are silk brocades and banners of faded silk, dark wood on the walls, the smoke and aroma of chalice-shaped yak butter lamps, golden images of Buddhas. Lamas in maroon and saffron robes sit in alcoves intoning from the scriptures. Against one pillar stands a broom. Against another a woman with a prayer-wheel leans in a trance. A thousand small Buddhas look down from niches in the wall. There are *tankas* showing demons tormenting their victims, and others of the building of the Potala. Men with daggers and rosaries force their way through the crowd. And above everything one can hear the deep clang of the bell whose frayed rope the pilgrims pull as they press past, and the endless chant of '*Om mani padme hum*'.

The pilgrims push slowly through the tiers, corridors, stairs, galleries, halls and chapels of the great labyrinth. They implant coins in wax over the doorways and drag their rosaries along the vermilion doors of closed rooms, pressing their heads against the dark gold dragon-shaped knockers. Monks attend to the lamps with strainers, tongs and trimmers. Dogs bark at rival dogs; children carry younger children on their backs. A woman weeps as if in agony and, when the corridor opens out into a hall, prostrates herself on the ground. At the end of the hall is an altar to a Buddha, top-knotted and long-lobed, an indescribable sense of peace on his unlined features. Before him offerings are placed: urns, peacock feathers, teapots, incense sticks, plastic gladioli, a sheet of red cloth, copper bowls, a glass paperweight, toffees, oranges, four yellow paper roses, coins brimming over in a bowl, a portrait of the Dalai Lama, a ceramic dog, a little grain. The golden statue itself is swathed in sashes – white, saffron, yellow – fastened to its robes with needles and safety-pins. A thermos flask and a red fire extinguisher stand by the door. The smell of incense permeates the dark rooms.

So fervid and overwhelming is the experience that when I am finally extruded into the sunlit exit, I find myself trembling. As I walk down the path along the unornamented white wall of the back of the Potala, beggars pluck at my coat, and I stumble. Someone thrusts a prayer flag at me. I sit down to collect my thoughts as the crowd flows past. Even when I am walking back to the guest house, there seem to be far too many people on the streets. Once inside the sanctuary of my room I cannot bring myself to venture out again till the next day.

The city of Lhasa stretches out along the north bank of the Lhasa River, a tributary of the Brahmaputra. The east-west axis of the city begins at the Jorkhan temple (in the middle of the octagonal hub of the old town), passes along People's Street and Liberation Street to the Potala, and from there continues along Happiness Street to the Norbulingka. The Drepung monastery (one of the three great monasteries near Lhasa – the Sera and the Gandian are the other two) lies several miles to the west of the Norbulingka. It is here that I am headed today.

The bus stop is near the Potala, in an area now mainly given over to government offices and shops, in no way different from those of Lanzhou. But in the immediate vicinity of the Potala a few, a very few Tibetan houses survive. Walls of white stone blocks rise upwards at a slight angle towards a dazzling blue sky. Children fly kites from windows bright with boxes of geraniums and fuchsias. When I get to the bus stop I see that there are only three buses a day down Happiness Street, and I have just missed one of them.

I walk for a while, then hitch a short lift with a Tibetan driver. He drops me off at the dirt road that leads up to Drepung. The white-walled and golden-roofed monastery is spread out in a broad and spectacular band along the lowest third of a hill. Slow-moving groups of pilgrims, some chanting mantras, climb through the terraced wheatfields, past the cairns of stones, past the outhouses. One of them gets a chisel out and carves '*Om mani padme hum*' on a stone. A woman halts to adjust the position of the child strapped to her back. The pilgrims, with their highboned sunburnt features, woollen dress, leather and jewellery, remind me of Incas, which is not strange, since they are extensions of the same racial group, both living at high, sunny altitudes and rearing animals.

Though I have actually come here to see the temples, murals and statues, my four or five hours at Drepung take on the character of an extended walk. From the foot of the hill to the monastery takes under an hour for even the slowest pilgrim. A touch of local mist snakes through the steep alleys and doorways, which give onto empty courtyards, mounds of rubbish and dilapidated woodwork. Then, set off from this scene of destruction, free too of the insinuating mist, a temple rises, restored to beauty after years of neglect. Inside, darkened already by the black smoke of yak-butter lamps are murals of Kali, many-armed, garlanded with skulls. Buddhas sit calm-eyed in the side-chambers of the hall. Monks, all of them old, chant hypnotically from the sutras. The interior of the temple is cool and spacious.

There are a number of temples of this kind, each one stately and impressive, scattered around Drepung, but to an outsider like me, who knows nothing of the minutiae of their significance, they are ultimately frustrating. My excuse about the fresh vision that ignorance brings to a complex environment now makes no sense to me. But it is too late to do anything about it.

On the hillside behind the temples are ruins of wood and clay. These reminders of the fury of cultural intolerance are so far beyond repair as to discourage even the thought of it. They have been left to the nettles and the occasional bright hoopoe; even the peach trees nearby, their small fruit green and diseased, have imbibed the bitterness of this place. Yet even here, painted on the rocks in a rainbow of colour, one can see the ever-present *'Om mani padme hum'*.

I take a different route going down Drepung, behind the buildings, along a deserted path by a stream. Here there are no pilgrims, just those people who live and work in the monastery: a boy who is carrying a message to one of the temples; two men moving a large piece of glass; a man washing monks' robes in a pool along the stream. An arch of pale pink roses tenderly indicates the entrance of an apple orchard. The ground is spangled with tiny, deep blue butterflies.

By the time I have got back to the road I am too tired to think of walking back to Lhasa. I try to hitch a lift but without success. After an hour of this, when twenty trucks and jeeps have passed me by, I walk over to a walled compound down the road. The guard at the gate tells me that there are no trucks from his unit going into the city today. But if I want a lift, I should wait here until he hails down a truck: he knows many of the drivers. Within ten minutes I am standing at the back of an open truck speeding towards Lhasa.

The guard's gesture is by no means exceptional. Time and again, with no thought other than kindness, people have helped me along in this journey. And this experience is merely a continuation of what I have felt throughout my travels in China: a remarkable warmth to the outsider from a people into whom a suspicion of foreigners has so long been instilled. Directions, advice, meals, encouragement: what makes travelling in China so delightful is that you rarely feel the want of goodwill among the people, or sense that they are too busy to help you find your way. More often than not you will be given instructions – 'Walk north, then turn east at the crossroads, and at the second traffic light turn north again for a block': all Chinese directions are given in terms of compass-points – and when, being a stranger with no prior idea of north and south you look bewildered, you will be taken personally to your destination, even if this is completely out of your guide's way. Protests are over-ruled with a smile. What is ironic is that the same obstructive bureaucrat who drove you to tears of frustration about an obscure regulation or a minor detail on a form may in his private life be so hospitable and generous as to bring you to tears of gratitude.

My companions on the truck are all Tibetan. Upon hearing that I am from India they question me closely about the welfare and whereabouts of the Dalai Lama, neither of which I am conversant with. One man, pointing to his old parents who are sitting on a spare tyre in the back of the truck, tells me they are determined not to die until they have seen the Dalai Lama again. There is some talk by the government that under certain circumstances he may return. But the former leader of a theocracy may be uneasy about returning to a home where he would now have no vestige of secular power.

I ask to be dropped off near the Norbulingka Park. Today is Thursday and I had hoped that the palace itself – the summer residence of the Dalai Lama – would be open. But it looks deserted. I am wandering around glumly when a small tourist bus draws up, and a door in the side of the palace wall opens. About fifteen mainly American tourists step out and are drawn in beyond the wall. I glimpse a garden beyond, and slip in with the rest of them, though I now look incongruous in my Chinese outfit and am afraid of being thrown out. Luckily I have my Nikon with me, so I flourish it furiously, taking photographs of unworthy cosmos and wilting dahlia as if my life depended on it. The Chinese guide seems puzzled but does not for the moment question my credentials. He speaks fluent English; his wry quips draw a smile even from the world-weary tourists. But I do not think much of the garden, which is totally lacking in imagination; nor indeed of the palace, which has too much of it. Italian chandeliers, paintings from Ajanta, Tibetan rugs, pictures of kittens and other diverse objects are assembled together, seemingly without connection or coherence. Some of them – the Buddhas, a mural of the Fifth Dalai Lama, so revered everywhere – are beautiful in themselves, but as we hurry through rooms ('This is where the Dalai Lama met high officials'; 'This is where he slept on the night before he fled to India'; 'This is where he meditated on esoteric Buddhism'; 'This is his bathroom'; 'This is his record player') my mind finds it difficult to react to the clutter of incompatible stimuli. It is like being force-fed onions with condensed milk.

The guide finally decides to ask me where I've come from, and I confess to my subterfuge. We get talking; Nanjing, as it happens, is his hometown. When the minibus is about to leave, he asks me if I would like a lift into town, or perhaps to go with them to the carpet factory, their next stop. He checks to make sure it's all right with the group leader, John. But as I am about to board the bus, a heavy-set woman hisses at me, so that only I can hear, 'How dare you get onto this bus with us; this is a Lindblad Tour, and we are paying more than ten thousand dollars for this trip.' I am so shaken by her remark that I am about to get off, but then John says, 'Hi! Get on – you're very welcome to join us,' and pushes me on. He hasn't heard her, and I decide to stay to prevent a scene. It is curious how wealth makes some people pleasant, by doing away with worry and petty frustration; and how it makes others abominable.

China is for the people in this group the last leg of a long tour of Europe and Asia. At the carpet factory they buy a number of small carpets, hand-woven and embossed in dragon and flower motifs. The one odd feature of this factory is the portrait of Mao that stares anachronistically down at the weavers as they work at their looms.

Later, when I bump into Norbu in the old town, I ask him about the Mao cult in Tibet: the badges, the displays, the portraits, the quotations. Why is Tibet so many years behind the political fashion? Norbu has never been outside Tibet, but those of his friends who have, have told him about the deMaoification so apparent in the rest of China; and one can of course tell, simply by reading the *People's Daily*, that apart from token obsequies, the cult has died away; more, that Mao has now been criticised as having made grave errors of policy and practice. Norbu says that the problem in Tibet is that the deification worked too well. Because of the precedent of the worship of the Dalai Lama, Mao is now seen by many as another god-king. It is thus difficult to dethrone him. This god, moreover, is a Han god; and what will Tibetans think of their Han rulers if they allow, not to say encourage, the denigration of this most potent symbol of their rule?

We walk around the octagon for a while, talking of this and that. We haggle with a pavement hawker about the price of a small Tibetan copper box, the size of a cigarette packet. Norbu brings it down from 25 to 6 yuan. The hawker also offers us silver dollars bearing the image of Yuan Shi Kai, the efficient and unscrupulous general who attempted, in the early years of the Republic, to restore imperial rule, with himself as emperor. There must be millions of such coins in Tibet. They sell at 12 yuan apiece here, and anyone can make his fortune in arbitrage by selling them in Guangzhou (Canton) at more than 50 yuan each.

Norbu asks me over to his house, which is close by. There is a rainbow across the street, arching outwards from a cloud. I stop to take a photograph. We walk to an intersection, and turn right into a maze of little lanes. His sister starts as we enter the courtyard, but recovers quickly. Their father is out, she says. She asks me to come in and sit down.

I look around the room. The furnishings are poor, but spotless: a long low table covered with a plastic tablecloth, a chest of drawers, a few chairs, a piece of thin cloth drawn across the window as a curtain. My eye settles on a picture of the Dalai Lama. I ask Norbu what he thinks of him; he seems ambivalent. 'My father and elder brothers are firm believers. For me he is a Tibetan leader, that's all.'

'Your mother?' I ask.

'She died some years ago,' he replies.

'Oh.' I try to change the subject, asking him about certain lamaist rituals and where and whether I can get to see them. As he is talking, an older man, tired but fiery, perhaps in his early forties, comes in. I do not recognise him from Sunday's picnic. He now speaks. 'A great deal has changed in the last few years. Even our own families don't understand our habits and our religion. The older people pray, the younger ones are unconvinced. But religious persecution is nothing new. Indian history, from what I have read, has its own share of it.'

I look at him. 'I am surprised you know so much about India,' I say.

'My elder brother knows a good deal,' says Norbu. 'As you can tell, his Chinese too is excellent, though at home we speak Tibetan.'

The sister brings in some tea. It is delicious, sweet and hot and milky like the stuff at home.

'Yes. Well,' I wonder out aloud. 'Do you think you would have a better regime if the Dalai Lama was back in power?'

Norbu looks keenly at me, a little surprised by the directness of the question. 'There isn't much point in thinking about that. Tibet is a part of China now, for better or worse. I wouldn't want to be ruled by priests. But to be ruled by the Hans isn't much better.'

His elder brother breaks in. 'Do you know what we have suffered, here, our family, because of the Chinese and their Cultural Revolution?' he asks. 'My father spent thirteen years in prison, and I spent twelve, because of them.' He looks at me with the arrogance of sorrow, then continues. 'An uncle of mine was killed when they invaded Tibet – and then their Cultural Revolution – you can't imagine what it did to our family. Our lives were ruined, mine and my father's – and my mother, when I think of her death, I can hardly bear to think of such things.'

He goes out into the courtyard for a while, and Norbu, calmer, says to me, 'He cannot bear it . . . Have another cup. I can see that you like it. It's the same with us. If a day passes without sweet tea, it doesn't seem complete.'

Children stray in and out of the room. A young boy, Zashi, eight years old or so, comes in and replenishes my tea from a thermos flask, then looking enquiringly at Norbu (who seems to be his uncle) disappears. When I get a chance to return to the subject, I ask Norbu what happened to his family.

He tells me about the imprisonment, the charge and the mock trial. 'Now at least we've been completely cleared but you cannot imagine what it was like for us during those years.' He turns to his sister. 'Bring the documents from the drawer.' I read them almost with disbelief. There are three of them, the final one being the document of exculpation. It was only after the issuance of this document, vindicating them, that the brother, and some months later the father, were released.

Norbu continues. 'My father came home. He was a wraith, not surprising, considering that during his years in prison he got only a couple of *liang* of *sampa* a day – not enough to fill even half that teacup. We sent food in, but it never got to him. When he was taken to jail, he had five children, the youngest just two years old. How could this child have any feeling for him as a father? I was ten when they took him away, and even I hardly remembered him. What bitterness my family suffered you cannot even begin to imagine. My mother, with four children to take care of . . . We couldn't get work – no-one would give work to the children of a counter-revolutionary. My father's parents had left us some money, and we went through it all. They were well off, but now nothing is left of all that except for a few cups and utensils. If it hadn't been for help from my uncle – my father's younger brother – we wouldn't have been able to go on. Look, you haven't eaten anything. Let me get you some noodles. They've already been cooked.'

I allow myself to be persuaded. His sister brings three bowls of noodles in. On the noodles are cubes of yak meat, and there is also a bowl of red chilli sauce.

After polite protestations, I begin eating. 'How often were you allowed to visit your father?' I ask.

Norbu, self-possessed until now, seems close to tears. 'Well, my father was in jail awaiting trial for three years, and then, after trial and sentence, served another ten. We did not see him once, not even at the trial, which took place in the Sports Stadium, and was watched by thousands of people. My mother was bed-ridden for those three years; on the day of the trial she couldn't even get up. There were 'activists' all around the neighbourhood. We children would have been stopped if we had tried to go. After the trial, and the sentence of eighteen years' imprisonment, our mother got worse and worse, and died within a few months. She never saw him again from the time he went to jail.'

He goes to a drawer, and brings out an old photograph. It shows a young couple with five children, a baby on the mother's lap, the mother herself smiling and the whole scene stable, domestic, and – if such attributes can be inferred from posed photographs – happy. I think back to the previous Sunday, when, in the park, I had had the same impression.

I point to the Tibetan writing above his father's head and ask him what it means. 'Nothing of importance,' he says.

'Is that you?' I ask, pointing to the serious-looking child who most resembles him.

'No, that's my other brother. You haven't met him. He isn't often here.' Norbu takes the picture and puts it back in the drawer.

We don't say anything for a while. Norbu wonders why his father is out so late: it is evening and he should have been back by now. I think of his father, and the picnic in Norbulingka a few days ago.

I turn to Norbu. 'You know, last Sunday when we met in the park, it seemed to me that you were the ideal happy family. How can you manage to forget, even for a day, what happened to you?'

He does not answer, and I do not follow up the question, and for a while sip my tea, which has been replenished. The sister appears quietly by my side and re-heaps my bowl with noodles. 'If I had known you were going to do that I would have covered my bowl,' I say, laughing. She smiles. 'You are being polite. This food isn't good. Our conditions are very poor, not like what you're used to.' The words, purely formulary Chinese, in her voice do not sound formulary. There is a noise at the gate; she goes to the curtains and peeps through, nervously. It is Zashi, the young boy, going out to fly kites with his friends.

'Are you afraid we're being watched?' I ask.

'No,' says Norbu. 'But the habits of thirteen years we can't change in three. It's different now; we can talk to you freely, you can come to our house, we aren't afraid. But a few years ago if you had talked to us, if you had even approached us on the street, we would have turned to avoid you. We couldn't dare to speak to a foreigner. We would be observed. The contact would brand us as counter-revolutionaries, unrepentant children of a counter-revolutionary.' He looks around at his elder brother and sister. 'In those days, you know, in this area, even the people on the streets would turn away when we went past, would pretend not to know us, children of counter-revolutionaries, even those we had thought of as friends. Now, of course, we have all been rehabilitated. My elder brother has got his job back after being cleared. Cleared.' He repeats the word bitterly. 'He spent three years awaiting trial; at least that was with my father, together. Then he was tried and sent to Lhasa Prison No. 2, sentenced to twelve years. My father was tried a few days later and sent to Lhasa Prison No. 1. Almost all the prisoners there were in for political crimes. They were treated worse than the real criminals. My father was guilty of "contradictions between the people and the enemy", while the murderers and rapists were only guilty of "contradictions among the people".'

'I must go,' I say. 'It's late.' But I sip my tea, and he carries on.

'We're safe now, but we are ruined. We have almost nothing. Most of what we had was confiscated, and we got 300 yuan as compensation for what happened to us. And as for the family, look at my eldest brother, grief-crazed. And my younger brother is like a madman: he wanders around here and there and can't do any work. My father, too – you saw him on Sunday and he seems fine, but mention my mother, and he can hardly speak for grief. And who can say, a year, or two, or five, and policies will change again and people will look at us as before. It's not just the Gang of Four who did this to us. But we can't mention names.'

I thank my hosts, refuse a seventh cup of tea, and put on my cap. 'Please come again before you leave Lhasa,' Norbu says. 'I'll be sure to,' I reply. 'Please give my regards to your father.' His sister leads me through the darkened lane to the main street where people are laughing and talking, and dogs barking at bicycles and each other. As I turn left, and west, I notice again the angled roofs of the Jorkhan, no longer gold but black against the early night sky, and high behind it two solitary bright stars, or perhaps planets. Between them is a light paper kite, rhomboid, tail-less, like the ones we have at home, a prisoner of string and wind, flying now in one direction, now in another, with no appraisable trend or endeavour.

14

Lhasa:

a ceremony near the Sera monastery

I wake up at half past five in the morning. It is still pitch-dark, and since it is summer, I am puzzled by this until I recall that, so far west, we are still on Beijing time. Dawn is two hours away. I put on all the warm clothing I have, take my torch with me and go out onto the street. Even the dogs are asleep. There is a pervasive misty drizzle. My eyes accustom themselves a little to the dark. To my left looms the huge tilting wall of the Potala.

As I walk, the cold seeps into me, and the drizzle, and the knowledge of the long walk ahead, and perhaps most of all the fear of what I am going to see. After half an hour I consider turning back but a mechanical sense of will takes over. The road to the Sera monastery is deserted; not a truck, not a pedestrian is out at this hour.

Slowly it grows lighter, and by the time the sky is grey with dawn, I have arrived at the place. My Tibetan friend has told me not to venture too close for fear of giving offence. I stay on this side of the stream. On the other side is a track leading to the rock, and above it the mountain-side rises sheer to the skyline. It is only later that I realise that the tiny saw-toothed serrations at the top are eagles, waiting.

The whole of the base of the mountain is obscured by thin smoke, so that at first I can make out nothing but the rock: a vast flat slightly sloping slab of stone. As the smoke shifts and returns, I discern a truck, a trailer, some wooden carts, and the movement of a few figures. Fires have been lit, and on the ground beside the trucks is a tent-like structure under which some people are crouching.

I have arrived during a pause in the work, which has already begun. It is about 7.45 by my watch, or about 5.45 in real terms. The men come

147

down to the stream to get water in plastic containers, then go back up to their fires to cook and eat breakfast. As it becomes lighter I see that there are human corpses lying on the rock, stripped and held in place by the head, while the lower torso, beginning from the legs, is hacked or cut up.

8.10. The men resume their work. One, clad in white and wearing a turban, seems to be the leader. They work with impressive speed, severing, chopping and mincing the meat. One young man in particular lops through the flesh and muscle and bone with marked vigour and despatch. His skill makes it possible almost to forget what it is he is cutting through. Above, on the skyline, the eagles have gathered. Sometimes family and friends of the dead come to watch the rites, but today I am the only one here.

8.20. The men have got to the upper body, and are working with a will. A few other people have joined me on my side of the stream. They are Han Chinese from Shanghai, who are in Lhasa on the adopt-a-district-in-Tibet scheme. They walk over to me, make a few jokes about the ceremony we are watching, then – laughing, talking, smoking – wade across the stream and approach the rock. They stand there, observing matters at close range. The man in the turban turns to look at them angrily. They get closer, and with insulting casualness, saunter up to the rock. One of them starts laughing. At this the turbaned man climbs down the rock and shouts at them in Tibetan, flinging a small bone down on the ground in front of them. They start, but do not leave their ground. The man then picks up a human leg that is lying on the rock, and chases them to the river, roaring with rage and brandishing it at them. They are terrified, and flee across the stream, one of them tripping and falling in. They now stand wet and trembling where they were a while ago.

8.50. The work goes on. The man in white stretches out his arms to the sky and utters a long cry. The eagles swoop down from the ridge and wheel in huge dark circles, lower and lower, finally settling on a small hill near the rock. One of them passes low over my head; there is a startling smell of decay. The huge birds sit, disciplined, on this hill, and are fed some preliminary scraps of meat by the man in white.

8.55. A tractor crosses the stream, and goes off to a village in the distance. The meat is now being mashed and mixed with barley-meal before being fed to the eagles. There are some that appear to be favourites.

9.00. An army truck comes down to where the Shanghai people are standing, and the soldiers get out and chat with them. They have brought what from this distance appears to be a telescope on a tripod, which they now have trained on the rock. The man on the rock is holding a large stone over his head with both hands. He brings this down again and again to smash the cloth-covered skulls. The eagles are eagerly observing the rock. One or two of them break formation, but are driven back. They stretch their curved beaks forward. Some sit with wings outstretched, as tall as a crouching man.

9.20 A monk wades across the stream towards the rock. He stands there in his maroon and yellow robes, and blesses the meal. The man in the white turban calls the eagles perched on the hill out onto the rock, and they set to. They are also fed by one of the men from a bag containing human mince mixed with *sampa*. The rock is now completely covered by the glutting birds.

9.50 The eagles are feeding. A crow joins them; they ignore it. I continue to watch, though now everyone has left. The army truck too has driven off.

10.10. The men working on the slab disperse. Three women cross the stream, and pass under the rock, which by now is cleaned of meat. The last of the birds flies off, up the slope and across the ridge. I get up and make my way to the nearby monastery of Sera.

My legs are unsteady after sitting in one position on the ground for such a long time. As I hobble along, a group of children standing on a small plank bridge wave at me and shout. I look towards Sera, but feel that rather than face a monastery after this experience, I would like to walk back towards Lhasa. I won't try to get a lift.

I walk back, thinking, and pause from time to time. The distant Potala looks lovely in the morning light; its less elaborate back face is towards me. The golden roofs glint, and the sky grows more and more blue. On the side of the road a couple of men, dismounted from their horse-carts, are cooking a meal on a fire blown by a bellows.

Christians and Muslims bury their dead, in effect feeding them to the worms. The Parsis feed their dead to the vultures in their Towers of Silence, but they leave the bodies whole. Here in Tibet, where wood is scarce and the ground hard for much of the year, the body is chopped up, mixed with meal, and fed to the eagles. Later I ask Norbu how common this rite still is; he says it is increasingly being replaced by cremation. He attended his uncle's funeral a year ago, however; that was of the kind I saw this morning. He felt queasy when they came to the head. I felt the same myself, though of course we Hindus also break the skull during the ceremony of cremation.

15

Lhasa: a final weekend

Lhasa is a smelly city, but was apparently worse before the public lavatories were improved. It hardly behooves an Indian to point out such features as rotting rubbish heaps; but one particular road, connecting Happiness Street with Construction Street, is completely covered with a green and malodorous scum, in which a dog has drowned. Every time I take a walk I notice the dog in the same position but in a more advanced stage of decomposition. Today it smells fouler than ever.

For the last few days, though I have tried to keep myself occupied, the exit visa has preyed on my mind. The tension of not knowing whether it will be granted, and of impotence in the face of the decision-making of others, makes me so jittery that I decide to go down uninvited to the Foreign Affairs Office yet again to enquire. Mr Ho isn't at the office, so I visit his home at the back of the compound. He has gone off to the airport to meet a group of tourists. Mrs Ho asks me to sit down and wait. She has just returned with the baby from Sichuan, where they lived for a year until she thought he would be strong enough to withstand Lhasa's rarefied air. Mr Ho must have missed them both a great deal. They live in a single long room, the rear half of which has been converted into a kitchen.

Mr Ho comes in, bearing a watermelon, and smiling from ear to ear, delighted to be back with his family. He is pleased to see me too.

'I was just about to go around to the guest house,' he exclaims. 'The police gave me back your passport today.' I open it quickly. Inside, opposite my exit visa, are the words: 'Allowed to exit China through Zhangmu, Tibet. By order of the Public Security Bureau, Lhasa.' I am at a loss for words.

Mr Ho cuts off my stuttered thanks with a 'Have you eaten? Why don't you have lunch with us?' and goes into the kitchen to help with the cooking. After a week of guest house canteen food, the delicately flavoured stew we eat is indescribably delicious. It is a convivial occasion, and I for one feel like a bird who, long confined in a room, all of a sudden finds a door in the glass wall, and flies out.

Being now at large, I sketch out a quick list of places I would like to see: the temple of Ramache, the Gandian Monastery, the towns of Gyangtse and Shigatse. They are all accessible now: Gyangtse and Shigatse lie on the road to the Nepalese border; the Gandian Monastery is a few hours by road and foot from Lhasa; and Ramache, clearly marked on the tourist map of Lhasa, is ten minutes' walk from the Foreign Affairs Office.

Ramache is a smaller temple than the great Jorkhan. So little does it look like a temple that I walk past it and have to be redirected back. A derelict hulk of unsteady woodwork, Ramache is a pitiful reminder of the devastation of the late 1960s. Through closed doors on the first floor I catch a glimpse of a huge grey-suited portrait of Mao in the hall. A picture of a soldier, a worker and a peasant standing together gazing forwards with indignant resolve graces the plastered wall in a sad caricature of patriotic and socialistic zeal. From the twisted and stripped roofs, a few boys fly kites. The wooden metal-tipped steps are rotting. Everywhere the people of Tibet are trying to restore what was destroyed, but there is a limit to what is possible. How long, I wonder, will it be before Ramache is restored?

As I walk away, I think of what I have heard about the Gandian monastery: black and white photographs of what it used to look like can be bought on the street: it was even more magnificent than Drepung. But in 1959 it was bombed into rubble. When members of the Dalai Lama's delegation – visiting Tibet a couple of years ago by invitation of the Chinese Government to discuss the question of his return – asked for permission to visit Gandian monastery, they were refused. They nevertheless took a bus from Lhasa, then walked for several hours, and eventually arrived. When they saw it they wept, and returned shortly thereafter to India. To say that the Tibetans are bitter about the destruction of their temples and monasteries gives no idea of the depth of their feelings. It is as if the Germans had destroyed every single cathedral, every single village church in Austria. It will not be forgotten, even though the people are now allowed to reconstruct the buildings up from the ruins.

I decide not to go to Gandian. I am sufficiently saddened by Ramache, and have no wish to be further disturbed.

The image of the Austrian cathedrals is borrowed from a German student, Jürgen, whom I met in the canteen of the Number One Guest House one afternoon. He had flown in from Chengdu a few days earlier. Returning from Ramache, I now bump into a haggard-looking couple, who study at Beijing University: they have just arrived. Giancarlo is Italian, Beatrix Austrian. We are astonished to see each other and discover that we have both travelled by the same route. They too hitched a lift from Liuyuan; they too thought that they were the only ones to have done so. Later the four of us sit in my room pooling experiences and rumours. Apparently there was also a Swedish student who hitched in from Xining, then went off in the direction of the Nepalese border; no one knows if he made it or not.

Giancarlo and Beatrix talk about their journey. They were ill, cold and famished most of the time, but seem to have enjoyed it in the same perverse spirit that I suppose I did. We are chatting happily on when the door opens, and in comes the very man we have been discussing: the Swede, Tomas, back from his excursion to the Nepalese border.

Tomas obtained his special permission to exit through Tibet by using a Nepalese visa obtained in Beijing as a lever. When he got to the border town of Zhangmu, he decided that he was too short of time and money to enter Nepal, so he began the journey back to Lhasa. He got a view of the north face of Mount Everest as he passed Dingri. He is now eager to go by bus or truck to Chamdo in Eastern Tibet, and from there find his way back to Chengdu and eventually Beijing, in time for the beginning of his course at the Central Academy of Drama. Though Tomas has travelled for longer than any of us, he has remained fit through rigorous adherence to a sound diet. Here in Lhasa he is living on yogurt and fresh vegetables. He has been allocated the second bed in my room: we talk till late. Despite his great diffidence, he is excellent company, and most knowledgeable about art and opera, both Chinese and Tibetan.

The two of us go together to look for a lift, he eastwards to Chamdo, I westwards to Shigatse and Nilamu. The Foreign Affairs Office is unable to help us. So is the Postal Service – I had supposed that they would have a vehicle going to Nilamu at least once a week. The Foreign Trade Office: no luck here, either. What else can we try? An army truck? A geological survey jeep? Perhaps, now that the bridge is down, there will be no vehicles going in that direction at all. Tomas suggests that we bypass the *lingdao* of the various units, and instead try directly at the place where trucks are loaded before a journey. There I am told that there may just possibly be a truck going via Shigatse to Nilamu within the next couple of days. Tomas is less fortunate: there are rumours that one of the bridges on the way to Chamdo has been damaged by floods.

The bus depot, however, has not yet cancelled its bus to Chamdo. It is due to leave at eight o'clock on Monday. Having no other option, Tomas buys a ticket. He is now seriously short of cash, and I have to overcome an almost desperate reluctance before he will allow me to lend him a little money for the onward journey. Now that I know I am going straight to Nepal, my own financial anxieties are at an end.

Mr Shah writes me a letter of introduction to use if I get across the border into Nepal. 'To whom it may concern ... please render all needed assistance ...' etc. He gives me a letter for his sons in Kathmandu, and wishes me good luck in finding a lift. I buy a beautiful cumbersome Tibetan lock. I visit the Potala again. I persuade myself to act on the assumption that a lift will come through tomorrow, and that this is therefore my last day in Lhasa. I take a walk towards the Sera monastery.

On my way back, I hear a bicycle bell ringing furiously behind me. I turn to see Sui. He dismounts, and for a few seconds we smile at each other without speaking.

'Why didn't you come to see me?' I ask. He had mentioned that I would probably be put up in the Number One Guest House, and that he would look me up when he got to Lhasa.

Sui pushes his hair back. 'I've been kept too busy by my unit lately,' he says. 'And it's quite a way out of town.' He looks tired. 'Have you got a lift yet?'

'As good as,' I reply. 'I should be out of Lhasa tomorrow or the day after.'

'Will you come back through Lhasa on your way back from India?' he asks.

'I doubt it. No, almost certainly not. In fact I don't know if I'll ever be in Lhasa again.' I pause. 'And you? Might you be in Nanjing next year? You mentioned something of the sort during the journey.'

Sui smiles. 'Give me your address anyway. Who can tell?'

I reach for a pen in my backpack, and come across a couple of packs of Zhonghua cigarettes. 'Ah, there's something else I meant to give you.'

'Too bad you're leaving so soon. I would have liked to ask you home,' says Sui. 'I myself will be leaving for Liuyuan in a couple of days. If the road's anything like it was . . .'

'Yes – how did you manage to get the truck out?' I ask.

'A couple of tractors got us out on the evening of the second day. We arrived in Lhasa at midnight.'

'What did your wife say about your fishing expedition?'

Sui rings the bicycle bell. 'Where are you off to, at the moment? The guest house?'

'Yes. And you?'

Sui gets onto his bike. 'Just to buy a few things at the market: meat, vegetables . . .'

'Fish?'

'Yes, that too,' he replies easily, and waves a cheerful goodbye.

'Goodbye, goodbye!' I shout after him. It seems too short a meeting. But then we are lucky that it took place at all.

16

Through Shigatse

On Monday morning Tomas and I walk over to the bus station below the Potala. The waiting-room contains pictures, drawn with what I hope is artistic licence, of the route to Chamdo. In one picture near the ticket counter, a bulky vehicle of dubious sturdiness is displayed driving down a mountain road at what looks like a one-in-three slope; a hairpin bend, with no barriers on its precipitous edge, lies directly in front of it. Tomas looks concerned but determined. I see him onto the bus which, despite the rumours we heard, is leaving on time.

The truck-loading station is a few minutes' walk away down Happiness Street. The manager rubs his hands together when he sees me. 'Yes, yes, there is a truck leaving for Nilamu tonight,' he says, anticipating my question. 'What's more, the road is now clear as far as Zhangmu, so it'll be going there, too. Now, as for the money . . .'

'Money?' I ask.

'Yes, money. I'll give you a ticket.'

'But isn't your truck going to Zhangmu anyway?' This is the first time I've been asked for money while hitch-hiking.

'You see,' says the manager, 'our lifts are not free. We charge people to travel in our trucks. It's like a regular ticket. But you'll be the only passenger.'

'Oh.' I pause to consider this. 'Can I stop from time to time to take photographs?'

Yes,' says the manager. 'From time to time. That'll be 35 yuan, and here is your ticket from Lhasa via Shigatse and Nilamu to Zhangmu.' He hands it over. 'The truck will pick you up at ten o'clock sharp this evening from the Number One Guest House. It's at this moment being loaded with goods bound for Shigatse.'

Ticket in hand and lighter both in heart and in pocket, I walk down to the Bank of China: a long walk through this lively and affecting city that is like a slow farewell. The Potala, more than a hundred metres high, rises to my left. I pass by the Foreign Affairs Office, the street of the dead dog, Ramache and the old town. At the bank, things move with their usual sloth and suspicion. It is only after intransigence and unpleasantness on both sides that my original exchange receipts are accepted, and I am allowed to reconvert most of my remaining yuan into dollars. Nepalese and Indian rupees will only be available closer to the border, at the bank in Zhangmu.

I walk for a while along the river. The colourful façades of houses, flowers on their sills; prayer flags hanging by the river bank; policemen in white on point duty by the army camp; even the neurotic chorus of dogs seems delightful to me now.

I go to visit Norbu again; it is a sad occasion: the chances of his travelling outside Tibet or of my returning to Tibet are slim. We share some *qingke* wine, and he wishes me a good journey. 'You should write a book about this,' he suggests.

'I'm keeping a log. Maybe something will come out of that.'

'If we're in it, change things so we can't be identified.'

'Yes. I'll do that.'

'But don't exaggerate.' He looks serious.

'No.' I laugh at his expression.

'When does your truck leave?'

'Tonight, at ten.'

'Wait a minute.' He goes inside and returns with a pack of homemade snacks. 'Take these with you.'

'Where is everyone else?' I ask.

'They've gone off to a friend's. You're lucky that I'm at home. I was studying English.'

I tell him about this afternoon's exchange at the bank and am gently chided. 'It doesn't pay to lose your temper. But I suppose foreigners can afford it.'

'I'm sorry I've missed meeting your father again.'

'I'll tell him. I hope we meet again. Have a good journey.'

'Goodbye.'

'Goodbye.'

I walk away quickly. Outside the Jorkhan a man sits by the road carving inscriptions on slate. I see an '*Om mani padme hum*', and buy it without thinking. I will now have to carry it across the border on my back.

At eleven o'clock at night I get a phone call. The truck has been delayed. I should be ready at nine in the morning. The next morning at nine I am again ready with luggage and ticket. At ten I begin concentrating on the small knot of flies in the guest house foyer. At eleven I go into the yard and play frisbee with the waiters. At 12.30 a jeep arrives to take me to the truck departure station. We are there in ten minutes. The original truck has developed engine trouble; the goods have been reloaded onto a different truck. The manager introduces me to Wu, the driver. He is about forty, Han, of average height, and from his expression, of more than average irritability. As I get into the driving cabin, he asks me shortly why I have taken so long to get here. He has waited more than an hour for me to arrive.

Our plan is to get to Shigatse tonight, and tomorrow through Nilamu to our destination, Zhangmu. The truck squeals and rattles continuously; it is also given to spasmodic attacks of wheezing. Wu has many of the attributes of his vehicle. A continuous patter of grumbling is broken only by jolts of exasperation bordering on frenzy. To some extent this is understandable: living with a truck one of whose doors swings open at odd moments, whose windows won't wind up, which has neither windscreen wipers nor rear-view mirrors, and which makes such an unnerving racket is, no doubt, an affliction. (But it is not, for instance, like living with an incompatible spouse; the faults are corrigible, and I can't understand why Wu hasn't corrected them.) I tune out his comments after a while; we communicate through a series of cigarettes from each other's packets.

With Lhasa a few miles behind us, the road loses its smooth surface. We drive along a narrow ledge above the Lhasa river, then, very briefly, along the Brahmaputra itself. Having crossed it, we climb slowly to a high pass, Kamba La, capped by a cairn and prayer-flags. The pass overlooks a narrow lake, more than fifty kilometres in length, exquisitely calm and blue. The weather too is glorious. Through the zoom lens of my camera I see a white bird – it looks like a tern – swoop downwards into the lake. Birds have kept us company throughout this journey: hawks fly along the road, magpies flash in the barley fields, orange-tailed sparrow-shaped birds dip down as they fly from branch to telegraph wire. In one tree by the road sit six or seven eagles, soundless and motionless, indifferent to the percussion ensemble hammering by.

As we descend towards Yamdrok Lake, past small stone huts and green pastures, a few premonitory drops fall out of a clear sky. By the time we are at the tapered end of the lake, the sky is overcast. Against this darkness, at a turn in the road, appears a snow-white peak so brilliant and so unexpected that I gasp aloud.

We climb into rain and sleet. Sheep with madder-coloured stains on their fleece stand bedraggled among the rocks. Yaks stare, then bolt in alarm. The mountainsides weep mud and slush into channels by the side of the road. Streams rush along at will. Glaciers appear on either side, reaching down almost to the road itself. The windows of the truck provide no protection against the weather. Wu is not amused.

At evening we descend into the Gyangtse valley. The panes of both windows have now slipped down completely into their grooves, so Wu ekes and threatens them out again. As we stand by the road in the failing light, a horseman clatters past. In the distance stands the fortress or *dzong* of Gyangtse, built on a large stump of rock on the broadening plain. Night falls, Wu grows quieter, and in a few hours we are in Shigatse.

At the registration window of the truckers' yard, while I am pondering whether or not to report to the police immediately, Wu has another short and rabid attack of bad temper. 'Oh shut up and sign,' he shouts. 'It's late enough as it is.' The other truckers look at us. I won't allow myself to reply. One more day with this creep, I think, that's all. I sign and go to our room.

A few minutes later, Wu comes in. 'I'm returning to Lhasa tomorrow,' he announces. 'You'll have to find someone else to take you to Zhangmu.'

I don't say anything, and continue to look at him for an explanation. It is not forthcoming.

'Why?' I ask at last.

'The road between Nilamu and Zhangmu has been ruined by floods again. I just heard the news from the other truckers.'

'But you can still go as far as Nilamu.'

'My cargo is for Shigatse. I was to unload here, drive the empty truck to Zhangmu, pick up some rice that arrived from Nepal two months ago and take it back to Lhasa. I can't go to Zhangmu now, so I'm turning back. Looks like you're stuck here,' he adds with satisfaction.

'I have to go on,' I say. 'Perhaps there are other trucks going to Nilamu. I'd better check up.'

'No other trucks are going to Nilamu. With the road to Zhangmu under repair, Nilamu is a dead end.' He looks at me with an expression of amusement.

'Are you sure no other trucks are going there?' I ask, concentrating on the facts rather than on my growing inclination towards violence.

'Yes.'

'Well then,' I say in as calm a voice as I can manage, 'I must insist that you do.'

'What do you mean, insist?' shouts Wu.

'I don't like to force you to make an empty run, but I have to leave China in three days, as my documents expire then.'

'Well, that's your affair,' says Wu.

'What do you mean, my affair?' I shout.

'Just what I said. Your affair, not my affair. Got it?' Our voices must be audible all over the Transport Yard.

'Do you mean to say,' I ask, now in a cold fury, 'that you won't honour the ticket issued by your own unit?'

'Ticket? What ticket?'

'Surely you must know that your unit sold me a ticket to Zhangmu.'

'I don't believe you.'

I hand him the ticket. I suppose that when the truck I was to travel in was changed, the manager must have forgotten to fully explain the situation to the new driver. This would account for a lot; for instance, why Wu felt he had licence to be surly and insulting. His eyes burn through the inconvenient piece of paper. He explodes: '*Ta-ma-de, ta-ma-de.* Anyway I won't go on until I have explicit instructions from Lhasa.'

Only by recalling Norbu's advice do I avoid a sympathetic detonation. It is now midnight. I tell Wu we'll solve this problem in the morning. I toss about, fuming and anxious, and cannot sleep for hours. How often of late have I been prone to these puerile bouts of rage.

In the morning Wu reiterates his stand. I go to the police station to try to extend my residence permit. They regret that they cannot do this. I ask if they could perhaps help me to get an alternative ride to Nilamu; but, to the best of their knowledge, there is none. Finally I suggest that they talk to Wu themselves. An officer comes down with me. Wu is recalcitrant, says he doesn't care, he didn't write out the ticket, the road is closed, he won't go. The officer assures him that I must leave China fast, and that the ticket obliges whoever is driving this truck to take whoever purchased the ticket to the destination mentioned on it – or at least as far as possible. Eventually we prevail. Once we have, Wu is less, rather than more, resentful towards me. In a sense, the responsibility has been taken off his shoulders. He continues to unload the truck, and I look around Shigatse until lunchtime.

Shigatse is the second largest town in Tibet, and the erstwhile seat of the Panchen Lama. The great *dzong* here has been destroyed (during the Cultural Revolution). Its vast blackened back wall, hundreds of feet high, stands against the mountainside. This is all that is left of the fortress. Across this wall there is a painted slogan, half-faded, too huge to be conveniently erased. This place looks as though it could not have been destroyed otherwise than by dynamite, but I do not enquire about the means. I enter the surviving area of the Zashilumpo monastery. An old lama, carrying three wooden tablets, shows me around in a most friendly way. Many visitors from other parts of Tibet roam through the temples and galleries, praying and chanting. The place has resumed a life of its own. Most impressive of all are the sutra rooms where the scriptures are kept; the interior hall where monks sit and meditate, chanting softly, very still, like a hundred aged statues; the macabre *tanka*s of Kali; and the great cymbal-drums, whose upper cymbal and attached drumstick synchronise the muffled thud and brilliant clang that sound through the resonating halls.

I open a tin of bayberries; Wu and I share it in silence. The ride to Nilamu starts at one o'clock. Wu has found another passenger, a soldier who is headed for Dingri. The three of us do not talk much during the journey. Occasionally I ask to take a photograph. There are electricity posts made from pillars of baked mud running from the main line across the plain to a village. On the mountainsides, white pebbles are arranged into slogans: 'Long live the Communist Party of China'. At a checkpoint near Dingri, my exit visa and endorsement to exit through Tibet are carefully examined. Late in the afternoon a furious rain begins, but we climb southwards and out of it towards evening.

We are now crossing the Himalayas themselves. Though the north face of Everest was covered by cloud when we passed it at Dingri, we are now at a pass where another great snow-peak Shishapangma (over 8,000 metres) is clearly visible. It is sunset, and the clouds twist and disperse around its pointed pinnacle with striations of pink and blue in the sky behind.

After the wheezing and squealing of the truck, there is suddenly silence as we freewheel down the pass of Thong La, steeply and swiftly off the edge of the Himalayas. Then darkness, a stretch of winding road, and after an hour the lights, level-terraced, of Nilamu.

17

Nilamu:

a day among waterfalls

Everywhere in the world climatic zones are arranged in latitudinal bands. A north-south journey is therefore likely to be much more varied than an east-west journey of the same length. In western China the main topographical features are also latitudinal, and this enhances the variety of a longitudinal journey. Thus sandy deserts have given way to basins and basins to cold plateau, aridity to pasture, pasture to glaciers, snow-peaks and high passes; and now suddenly I am in a rapid southwards descent to the warm foothills of the Indian subcontinent.

The descent could not have been more abrupt. From the Thong La pass, over 5,000 metres high, to Nilamu and Zhangmu, a little over 2,000 metres, is a change from alpine meadow to semi-deciduous forest. As I begin walking down from Nilamu to Zhangmu midges bite my ankles. The Bhotakoshi rages far below, the sun shines calmly above – through, for the first time in a fortnight, generous levels of air. I have far too much luggage, and though I have roped some of it onto my back it is an inconvenience whenever I wish to take a photograph.

This valley, draining southwards towards the Ganges, has eaten deeply into the Qinghai-Tibet plateau. It is thus surrounded on three sides by tall peaks. In fact the high terrace of Thong La through which we crossed the mountains before Nilamu lies considerably to the north of the main range of the Himalayas. From the high green walls of the Bhotakoshi, waterfalls drop hundreds of feet down to its surface: cascades and cataracts, twisting through plaited undergrowth or plunging straight down slabs of rock. The road folds back on itself or skirts around the edge of the hills in a continuous downward slope towards Zhangmu.

The tributaries of the river, when they are not actually waterfalls, rush down their angled gradient with an impetus terrifying for streams only a few metres across. The flood that struck here a few days ago has destroyed a small bridge on one such stream. Standing by the stream, its brown waters frothing a couple of steps away, its boulder-spattered spray striking my clothes and my face, I look down the thirty-degree slope that leads it to the Bhotakoshi a few hundred metres below. The stream roars through a gorge jammed with tree-trunks, rocks, debris. The walls of the gorge, ravaged by what must have been an enormous volume of water, show that the flood level at the height of the damage was thirty metres above even its present flow.

Every few minutes the troubled skin of the stream bursts open with new force against the rocks or the lashed logs which some roadworkers are trying to ease across it. A road-bridge here has been swept away, cutting Nilamu off from Zhangmu. At the moment there is only a makeshift bridge of logs, shaking on its rocky supports a few feet above the stream, with a cable on each side for a hand-grip. Though it is not more than five metres across, a slip would mean instant pulverisation. I hesitate to cross with my unbalanced luggage, but there is no choice. Finally I gather courage from an eight-year-old Tibetan child who walks, nonchalantly swaying with the cables, over to the other side.

Along the main valley the devastation is apparent high above the Bhotakoshi's current flow. The firm concrete bridge between Nepal and China has disappeared, as has the checkpoint which used to be above it. Huge chunks of the road have been scooped away. Small huts, terraced fields clinging to the almost vertical walls of the gorge, standing crops, trees, rocks, everything was ground down to what villagers describe as a black slurry. The violence of the rains helped loose some of the compacted snows in the glaciers above, thus bloating the river with the stored precipitation of previous years. Here in Tibet only property was destroyed in the flood but lower down in Nepal a number of lives were lost, especially when the river swelled at night.

From far above, their source invisible above the green walls, the waterfalls empty themselves into the Bhotakoshi. Some, white, turbulent, resounding, scramble down the precipitous incline in short spasms of interrupted energy. Others plunge directly down, thundering into pools of rock and fern, bamboo, bramble and pine. One falls over the road itself, which crawls for a distance under a ledge.

I plan to be in Zhangmu before nightfall; there is time to pause along the way. I have still got some of Norbu's snacks; I eat them and an apple sitting at the end of a small spur. At this point I can count no less than eight waterfalls, bright silver in the noon light. It is difficult to imagine this view without them, and yet they are guests of just one season: when the monsoon passes they too will disappear.

> 'A land of streams! some, like a downward smoke,
> Slow-dropping veils of thinnest lawn, did go –'

And across the valley against the grey verticality of a cliff a thin strand of water indeed vanishes into a mist or smoke atomised by the wind, to reappear, reconstituted from, it seems, the air itself into a liquid skein of light. There is enchantment in flowing water: I sit hypnotised by its beauty – water, the most unifying of the elements, that ties land and sea and air in one living ring. It has a channelled flow, unlike air, and its cycles are vaster, accepting all three states in nature. Snow and ice lie packed, perhaps for years, on the crests and cwms, in glaciers, in the permanent snows, suddenly to crack and thaw and churn into the snowmelt. The water, deeper than the highest peaks are high, lies in the sea until welled to the surface and accepted into the air as vapour. The moist air circles the world to fall again into the sea as snow or rain; or as snow or rain on the land.

'Highest good is like water,' says Lao Tzu. 'Because water excels in benefiting the myriad creatures without contending with them and settles where none would like to be, it comes close to the way.' . . . 'In the world there is nothing more submissive and weak than water. Yet for attacking that which is hard and strong nothing can surpass it.' Tasteless, it accepts all tastes, colourless, all colours, reflecting the sky, refracting the white stones of its bed, dissolving or suspending the soils and minerals over which it flows. The pulse of our bodies is liquid, as indeed all living pulses are. Water dissolves the salt of the parable in the Upanishads, covers the land of Genesis and flows by the paradise of the

Koran. And the random blur of noise, the tumult of light at which I now stare is the author of more beauty even than itself: cirrus and cumulus, rainbow and storm cloud, the strata of sunset, the indescribable scent of the first rains on the summer-baked plains.

'It is all in the water': Scotch whisky, Longjing tea. The universal element, it is yet so particular about its local excellences. It 'benefits the myriad creatures', yet the vehement loveliness of the cataract is the cause of flood and death in the overburdened stream below. Its substance yields to the guiding rocks, yet its form outlives the rocks that direct and hinder its flow.

I will during my life be certain to drink some molecules of the water passing this moment through the waterfall I see. Not only its image will become a part of me; and its particles will become a part not merely of me but of everyone in the world. The solid substances of the earth more easily cohere to particular people or nations, but those that flow – air, water – are communal even within our lives.

With this curious thought, I gather up my luggage again and set off down the road. Why, I wonder, do we stare so fixedly at water – at the sea, at waterfalls, at streams? It seems perverse when the land is so much more colourful, manifold, various. It is, I suppose, simply that water moves while the land is static – or rather that its movements, the putting out of leaves, the movements of the earth's crust, are imperceptible to us. It is this visible movement of water, whether of the concentric ripples on a lake, or of the 'sounding cataract' falling whitely into chaos, that informs the purity of a uniform element with the varying impulse of life.

18

Into Nepal

Zhangmu is a small settlement clinging to a hillside above the river. Its buildings are beaded along the road which zigzags down the slope: barracks, a guest house (where I have got a room), a shop, a bank, a few huts and a customs checkpoint. Across the river from the guest house lies Nepal, inaccessible now that the Friendship Bridge has been washed away. I will have to walk down-river until I find a bridge that is still standing.

Having changed my last few yuan for Indian and Nepalese rupees, I find that I have nothing left to do except to get a guide. The manager of the guest house introduces me to Tenzingtomang, a short and sturdy barefooted Sherpa. Tenzing sizes me up shrewdly but cheerfully, deciding what daily rate to charge me. He will carry part of my luggage, and our food and lodging on the way will be the same. The route leads through the hills and forests to Chaku, then through fields and along the river to Bahrbise. At Bahrbise we can cross the river on a bridge, arrive at Lamasangu within an hour, and take a bus to Kathmandu. It should take us three days to get there, says Tenzing, smiling encouragingly at the rain pouring down outside.

Tenzing looks less cheerful the next day: the weather is fine. I buy a gunny bag from the guest house. It used to hold rice; now it holds part of my luggage. At the customs post an official looks at it thoughtfully.

'Are you carrying any gold?' he asks me.

He gives my bag a perfunctory check, then takes my passport into another room for stamping.

Several people are waiting to be processed by customs, some coming from, some going to Nepal. A twenty-six-year-old woman, tired after spending four days walking from Lamasangu, but with an expression of quiet and compelling radiance on her features, sits opposite me. I learn that at the time of the Chinese entry in 1959, her parents sent her out of Tibet; she was then only five years old. She lived in India until a few years ago, when she moved to France. A friend of hers had very recently brought her news of her parents, whom she had asked him to trace in the old town in Lhasa. Now that the government permits close relatives to visit each other, she has come back to Tibet by plane, by bus and on foot. Several days of travelling lie ahead of her, and, perhaps, unforeseen difficulties. But all difficulties will, I'm sure, melt away before those compassionate and determined eyes.

Jigme, a shopkeeper from Kathmandu, who is also Tibetan by birth, introduces himself. He too is going to Nepal; perhaps we can keep each other company. He has travelled this route before, and exudes a happy confidence; an air enhanced by a bush shirt, shorts and a light backpack. Jigme speaks Tibetan, Nepali and English with great fluency; but the first transaction I see him involved in is conducted in complete silence.

Our passports are stamped, and we have just left the final Chinese checkpoint when we are halted by a soldier with a rifle. He looks closely at Jigme but does not challenge us. Just a hundred yards further on, while we are pausing to admire a waterfall, the soldier runs up to us again, looks quickly around, points to Jigme's watch, rolls out a wad of cash from his pocket, and makes a totally illegal purchase for 140 yuan.

The actual border with Nepal on this bank of the river is still some hours away. We walk at a fair pace: Tenzing steadily, step after step with great deliberateness; Jigme in a comfortable mixture of speed and rest; I in alternate modes of hyperactivity and collapse. We leave the road for a few minutes after Zhangmu to climb a steep track: we climb and climb until I can bear it no more. It is sunny, and a little before noon, but the path is still exceedingly slippery. My rubber-soled tennis-shoes and too-flexible green bamboo walking-stick make a hazardous combination. Whenever I slip, Tenzing views me balefully. He speaks no English or Chinese, I no Tibetan or Nepali. When the strain of silence becomes too intense, he breaks into an improvised Hindi – *garbar karta hai, ekdum slip* (make confusion, completely slip); or *rasta bahut badmash* (path very rascal) – which proves something I have often thought: that those who don't know a language properly are often most expressive in it. I remember an Italian friend who once asked me whether I planned to go by road or by 'the fluvial way'.

Increasing shade and cloud temper the earlier heat. We are now walking on the level, or downwards, into a country of bamboo, iris and rhododendron. We cross several streams, a log or two flung across them as bridges. Where the current is not too swift, I step, shoes and all, into the shallows to keep my feet cool. If I were on my own, I would probably walk a lot slower, and pause a lot more. The pace of our forced march is such that I decide not to take any more photographs for a while.

The forest clears, and we are in a small millet-growing settlement: three or four huts and a few cows. We buy yogurt, eat it with parched rice and sugar: for dessert we have some of my long-preserved, half-melted chocolate. We will soon be in Nepal, but for the moment we are clearly still in China: a poster of the young Mao is attached to the inside of a door.

We traverse a smooth, meadow-green yet almost vertical slope, hundreds of metres above the river. It is clothed with a lush, clinging grass, and lovely wild flowers. The path here is dangerously narrow. Whenever my attention strays, Tenzing warns me to watch my foothold – 'or you'll end up in Kakopani Hot Springs.'

Jigme pulls a number of leeches off my shirt as we pass through the moister regions near streams. The mites and midges are increasingly bloodthirsty. Fern, moss, nettle and bamboo merge into a patchwork of different greens.

A woman wearing a sari is washing clothes in a small stream. She looks up at us as we cross. The forest continues beyond. Suddenly a man steps out from behind a tree.

'Stop,' he says to Tenzing. 'Put that bag down.' He speaks in Nepali. I look at him, wondering what this is all about. Tenzing and he stare at each other. The man doesn't look like a robber; besides, he isn't armed.

'Who are you? What is your business with us?' I ask him in Hindi. 'The luggage he's carrying is mine.'

'I am a Government of Nepal customs officer,' replies the man in excellent Hindi. 'I must check your luggage. Are you an Indian citizen?'

'But I didn't know we had crossed the border,' I say.

'That stream there, that's the border. You've just crossed it.'

'That . . .?' I look back at the stream. The woman is wringing out clothes over the water. Her soap lies on one rock, her washing on another. She couldn't care less which country she is in. This is the first time a customs officer has stepped out from behind a tree to announce himself. 'There's no checkpoint here. How do I know who you are?' I demand. 'You aren't wearing a uniform.'

The man looks at me meditatively. 'Well, the checkpoint is up there on the hill. If you have any doubts I could go over your luggage there. Quite thoroughly.'

I give in. I open my bags by the forest path, and lay my books, clothes and camera on the stones, while the man looks interestedly on.

'You smoke a lot of cigarettes,' he comments. Several packets of 555 and two of Zhonghua lie among my possessions.

'Oh, I don't really smoke,' I say. 'These cigarettes are for other people.'

The officer does not object to anything I am bringing in with me. 'Let me help you put these things back,' he says. As he puts the articles in one by one, he casually places a packet of Zhonghua aside on the rock.

I get up to go, and equally casually pick up the packet and put it into my pocket. I am taking the Zhonghua back home specifically for my brother. The officer would have done better to have chosen a packet of 555s.

We move on, through field and hamlet and uninhabited tract. Jigme has gone on ahead. I feel a renewed energy, and walk more quickly. Tenzing brings up the rear in unflagging, unquickening steps. An hour later, I find Jigme halted near a schoolhouse in a small village, drinking tea. We wait for Tenzing. When, after fifteen minutes, he has still not arrived, I retrace my steps, and find him in the clutches of three gleeful officials who are going through my bags with unconcealed delight. 'Why didn't you stop *me*?' I ask. 'I'm also carrying things.' They ignore me.

'I told them these things had already been checked,' says Tenzing in broken Hindi.

'No one told you to speak,' snaps the youngest and most avid of the three officials.

I take out the letter from the Consul-General in Lhasa. Aggression dissolves in apology. They insist on helping me repack my things. I later discover that three packets of cigarettes (including one of the precious Zhonghua packs) have disappeared.

We have now descended to the Bhotakoshi: muddy, white-brown, fed by streams and snow-white waterfalls, sea-like in the way it pours over rocks, and terrifying in the way it has flooded to annihilate huge chunks of the road. At one place, there is nothing but a steep black slippery slope where the hillside has crumbled onto half the road, the other half having been gouged out by the river. We climb over this barrier into the hills again.

Everywhere there are signs of destruction: flooded crops, uprooted trees, collapsed roofs, broken walls, We halt on a slope in sight of Chaku, the night's resting-place. We are too tired to talk. I strip to the waist and squeeze the sweat out of my vest. Below the high convex slope on whose crest we are sitting is a confluence of a large stream with the Bhotakoshi; and Chaku lies just before it. Beyond Chaku, a bridge crosses the tributary; we are still on this side of the main river. We survey Chaku: a few houses strung out along the broken road below. One of them is Tenzing's home. He nurses his bare feet.

I take the zigzag slope down to Chaku in a series of controlled falls. Jigme finds a place for us to spend the night cheaply, while Tenzing goes home. We have a good dinner of dal and rice cooked by our landlord's family, then sleep upstairs on straw mats laid out beside bundles of chopped wood.

Outside the river roars, and a cool breeze blows the scent of smoke and cowdung through the open window. Then we hear rain, and the distant barking of a dog on the hillside, and the song of a cricket from a pile of firewood in a corner.

This would all be idyllic if the mosquitoes, mites, fleas, lice and bloodsuckers that infest this place did not make sleep an impossibility. With malevolent pertinacity they seek out even the smallest areas of exposed flesh. The lozenge-shaped red bloodsuckers are the worst.

When I finally manage to fall into a fitful sleep, it is only to be woken again by Jigme's furious cries as he tears and scratches at his arms. Shortly afterwards he drops off to sleep again, but now I cannot.

I fold my favourite shirt under my head as a pillow, and think of San Francisco and London, Nanjing and New Delhi. Oh my beautiful comfortable longsleeved cotton rough tough blue large-checked Pan-Am $100-compensation-for-loss-of-luggage shirt, how I love you. Levi, $15. How glad I am, O self-stitched, button-lost shirt, that I bought you and that I have brought you here with me.

We have made excellent time. A trek that in worse weather could have taken three days will probably be over by noon today. At five in the morning we set out from Chaku. Jigme tells me that the bus from Lamasangu leaves at two in the afternoon, so I feel no compulsion to be energetic.

The river pushes stones against each other with a deep grinding noise. A bluish-white stream flows into its brown spate. Nearby, a small watermill rests at the edge of the stream. A broken footbridge dips into the river.

The landscape is now increasingly familiar to me: terraced fields of rice, banana trees, flame-of-the-forest, *champa*. I see a piece of indigo-coloured paper fluttering by the side of the path. It is the covering of a packet of matches, of the sort in use in India and Nepal. Two women in bright saris walk through the emerald fields. As we enter Bahrbise, I notice the shops full of brilliantly coloured cloth and bangles. Even the police station (with its brightly painted motto: 'Truth, Service, Protection') has a clay elephant in front, decorated with a bowl of portulacas. One of the things I have been seriously deprived of for most of this year is colour.

Here, for the first time, a bridge over the Bhotakoshi has held. The river is broad now; there is a dam a few kilometres below. We cross the river, at last. The road once more turns into slush. Human labour and earth-moving machinery attempt to open it to vehicular traffic, but it is no easy task with landslides every few hundred metres. Finally, in the early afternoon we get to Lamasangu, from where, we are happy to hear,

the road to Kathmandu is still open. Actually, Tenzing is a bit upset that
the journey has only taken two days. He frowns as I count out his money,
and dumps the gunny bag unceremoniously onto the ground. But after
eating lunch with us and extracting a tip from me, he goes off more
cheerfully. I stuff the luggage I have been carrying into the gunny bag,
and haul the load down the road to the bus stop.

As we bump along the red-soiled valleys towards Kathmandu, details
of colour and shape leap to my eye. The last time I was home in India was
three years ago. This is the first time I have been to Nepal, but there are
many similarities to other valleys in the Himalayan foothills: Dehradun,
for instance, where I spent my high school years. These things now
affect me more powerfully than I could ever have imagined: small blue
hedgeflowers of a type I recognise but cannot name; lantana bushes; *sal*
forests; water-buffalo; trucks copiously ornamented with religious sym-
bols and hopelessly overloaded with worldly goods; bands of red chillies
spread out to dry on the ground and on rooftops; khaki-clad policemen;
ramshackle villages clustered around their temples; the bright clothes
and familiar features of the people; a woman selling cucumber and
chutney to the passengers at a bus stop. I even enjoy the characteristic
snorting and coughing of the bus as it clambers up and down the hills on
its five-hour journey to Kathmandu.

Kathmandu; Delhi

I get a cheap room in the centre of town and sleep for hours. The next morning, with Mr Shah's son and nephew, I visit the two temples in Kathmandu that are most sacred to Hindus and Buddhists.

At Pashupatinath (outside which a sign proclaims 'Entrance for the Hindus only') there is an atmosphere of febrile confusion. Priests, hawkers, devotees, tourists, cows, monkeys, pigeons and dogs roam through the grounds. We offer a few flowers. There are so many worshippers that some people trying to get the priest's attention are elbowed aside by others pushing their way to the front. A princess of the Nepalese royal house appears; everyone bows and makes way. By the main gate, a party of saffron-clad Westerners struggle for permission to enter. The policeman is not convinced that they are 'the Hindus'. A fight breaks out between two monkeys. One chases the other, who jumps onto a *shivalinga*, then runs screaming around the temples and down to the river, the holy Bagmati, that flows below. A corpse is being cremated on its banks; washerwomen are at their work and children bathe. From a balcony a basket of flowers and leaves, old offerings now wilted, is dropped into the river. A stone image of a Nandi bull sits firmly between two competing *sadhus*, each muttering his mantra, each keeping a careful but hopeful eye on the passers-by. A small shrine half protrudes from the stone platform on the river bank. When it emerges fully, the goddess inside will escape, and the evil period of the Kaliyug will end on earth.

At the Baudhnath stupa, the Buddhist shrine of Kathmandu, there is, in contrast, a sense of stillness. Its immense white dome is ringed by a road. Small shops stand on its outer edge: many of these are owned by Tibetan immigrants; felt bags, Tibetan prints and silver jewellery can be bought here. There are no crowds: this is a haven of quietness in the busy streets around.

In Kathmandu I wind down after my journey. I luxuriate in my tiredness; drift deliciously along, all energy spent, allowing sight to follow sight, thought to follow thought, for now (apart from the easily fulfillable intention of returning to Delhi) there is nothing, no intermediate step that I must perform: there is no lift to look for, no hill to climb, no load to carry, no town en route. There are no papers that I have to obtain. For a person of fundamentally sedentary habits I have been wandering far too long; a continuously wandering life like Sui's would drive me crazy. I marvel at those travellers who, out of curiosity or a sense of mission, wander through unfamiliar environments for years on end. It requires an attitude of mind more capable of contentment with the present than my own. My drive to arrive is too strong. At many points in this journey, impatience has displaced enjoyment. This tension is the true cause of my exhaustion. When I am back in Delhi I will not move for a month, just sit at home, talk with my family and friends, read, rewind, sleep.

Kathmandu is vivid, mercenary, religious, with small shrines to flower-adorned deities along the narrowest and busiest streets; with fruitsellers, flutesellers, hawkers of postcards and pornography; shops selling Western cosmetics, film rolls and chocolate; or copper utensils and Nepalese antiques. Film songs blare out from the radios, car horns sound, bicycle bells ring, stray cows low questioningly at motorcycles, vendors shout out their wares. I indulge myself mindlessly: buy a bar of Tobler marzipan, a corn-on-the-cob roasted in a charcoal brazier on the pavement (rubbed with salt, chilli powder and lemon); a couple of love story comics, and even a *Reader's Digest*. All this I wash down with Coca Cola and a nauseating orange drink, and feel much the better for it.

I discover that Indian currency is accepted on the Kathmandu streets at an exchange rate of 1.45 Nepalese rupees per Indian rupee. The Chinese exchange rates at the bank in Zhangmu were 0.149 yuan per Nepalese rupee and 0.162 yuan per Indian rupee. It occurs to me that the disparity in cross-rates could enable any habitual border-hopper to realise a tidy profit.

Using Indian currency to pay for a map of Nepal makes me feel quite dislocated. I consider what route I should take back home. If I were propelled by enthusiasm for travel *per se*, I would go by bus and train to Patna, then sail up the Ganges past Benares to Allahabad, then up the Jumna, past Agra to Delhi. But I am too exhausted and homesick; today is the last day of August. Go home, I tell myself: move directly towards home. I enter a Nepal Airlines office and buy a ticket for tomorrow's flight.

I look at the fluteseller standing in a corner of the square near the hotel. In his hand is a pole with an attachment at the top from which fifty or sixty *bansuri*s protrude in all directions, like the quills of a porcupine. They are of bamboo: there are cross-flutes and recorders. From time to time he stands the pole on the ground, selects a flute and plays for a few minutes. The sound rises clearly above the noise of the traffic and the hawkers' cries. He plays slowly, meditatively, without excessive display. He does not shout out his wares. Occasionally he makes a sale, but in a curiously offhanded way as if this were incidental to his enterprise. Sometimes he breaks off playing to talk to the fruitseller. I imagine that this has been the pattern of his life for years.

I find it difficult to tear myself away from the square. Flute music always does this to me: it is at once the most universal and most particular of sounds. There is no culture that does not have its flute – the reed *neh*, the recorder, the Japanese *shakuhachi*, the deep *bansuri* of Hindustani classical music, the clear or breathy flutes of South America, the high-pitched Chinese flutes. Each has its specific fingering and compass. It weaves its own associations. Yet to hear any flute is, it seems to me, to be drawn into the commonalty of all mankind, to be moved by music closest in its phrases and sentences to the human voice. Its motive force too is living breath: it too needs to pause and breathe before it can go on.

That I can be so affected by a few familiar phrases on the *bansuri*, or by a piece of indigo paper surprises me at first, for on the previous occasions that I have returned home after a long absence abroad, I have hardly noticed such details, and certainly have not invested them with the significance I now do. I think it is the gradualness of my journey that has caused this. With air travel the shock of arrival is more immediate: the family, the country, the climate all strike with simultaneous impact, so that the mind is bewildered, and the particular implications of small things obscured.

As evening comes on I walk to the Maidan, the open grass-covered common in the centre of Kathmandu. Goatherds drive their goats between the football players and the goal. The last overs of a cricket match are interrupted by a group of elder citizens taking a stroll across the pitch. I walk back to the hotel.

At 3.30 at night I am woken by insects. At five I am woken by the cooing of pigeons outside my window. At six I am woken by my alarm clock. I take a taxi to the airport. The plane is delayed, but by eleven o'clock we are airborne. Below lie the green hills of Nepal; in an hour I will be home. It will be the first time that my parents, my brother, my sister and I have been together in seven years. The family does not know where I am: I later discover that the telegram from Lhasa never did get to Delhi.

As I sit in my seat sipping tomato juice and adjusting my watch to New Delhi time, the whole of the last two months takes on a dreamy quality. I can more easily see myself standing outside the police station at Turfan than travelling through Anduo or Shigatse. Even having been to Tibet, it still strikes me as 'somewhere I would like to travel to', a place I feel I still know next to nothing about; yet I cannot imagine, once I am no longer a student, that I will ever have the means to return.

Almost to reassure myself that this journey did take place, I recite an incantation of names: Turfan, Urumqi, Liuyuan, Dunhuang, Nanhu . . .– the images regain substance –. . . Germu, Naqu, Lhasa, Shigatse, Nilamu, Zhangmu, Lamasangu, Kathmandu. But alongside these names there are others – Quzha, Sui, Norbu – that mean even more to me. I recall Quzha's comment: 'I'm glad things have improved in our relations.' It is a curiously innocent remark in a world where foreign relations are determined by little other than realpolitik.

If India and China were amicable towards each other, almost half the world would be at peace. Yet friendship rests on understanding; and the two countries, despite their contiguity, have had almost no contact in the course of history.. Few travellers have made the journey over the Himalayas, and not many more have made the voyage by sea; trade, while it has existed, has always been constrained by geography. In Tibet and South East Asia we find a fusion of the two cultures; but the heartlands of the two great culture zones have been almost untouched by each other. The only important exception to this is the spread of Buddhism.

Unfortunately I think that this will continue to be the case: neither strong economic interest nor the natural affinities of a common culture tie India and China together. The fact that they are both part of the same landmass means next to nothing. There is no such thing as an Asian ethos or mode of thinking.

The best that can be hoped for on a national level is a respectful patience on either side as in, for instance, trying to solve the border problem. But on a personal level, to learn about another great culture is to enrich one's life, to understand one's own country better, to feel more at home in the world, and indirectly to add to that reservoir of individual goodwill that may, generations from now, temper the cynical use of national power.

We touch down in Delhi at noon. The customs officer looks dubiously at the rice sack I am carrying over my shoulder and at the bottle of Glenfiddich I hold in my hand.

'Anything to declare?' He looks at the bottle.

'No. I got this at the duty free shop in Kathmandu.'

'Please open that . . . thing.'

I place the gunny bag on the counter, and take out the objects inside, one by one, like Santa Claus. He passes his hand gingerly over the stone with '*Om mani padme hum*' inscribed on it. He taps my soap-box thoughtfully. The photographer-bear goes through his paces, raising his camera and flashing away at the other now perturbed passengers. The customs officer looks at the bear with distaste.

'All right. You can go.'

I am home in half an hour.

Vikram Seth was born in India in 1952. He took his undergraduate degree in philosophy, politics, and economics from Oxford University, and was a graduate student at Stanford and Nanjing universities, where he studied the economic demography of China. He is the author of a book of poems, *All You Who Sleep Tonight*, and a novel in verse, *The Golden Gate*. His most recent novel is *A Suitable Boy*.

VINTAGE DEPARTURES

The Road From Coorain by Jill Ker Conway

A remarkable woman's exquisitely clear-sighted memoir of growing up Australian: from the vastness of a sheep station in the outback to the stifling propriety of postwar Sydney; from untutored childhood to a life in academia; and from the shelter of a protective family to the lessons of independence and tragedy.

"A small masterpiece of scene, memory...this book [is] the most rewarding journey of all."
—John Kenneth Galbraith

Autobiography/0-679-72436-2/$10.00 (Can. $12.50)

Looking for Osman: One Man's Travels Through the Paradox of Modern Turkey
by Eric Lawlor

As he traverses Turkey in search of exotic splendor recorded by nineteenth-century romanticists, Eric Lawlor finds instead a modern, professional, sometimes brutal land, with unexpected remnants of the old Turkey to be encountered along the way.

A Vintage Original/Travel/Adventure/0-679-73822-3/$11.00 (Can. $14.00)

A Year in Provence by Peter Mayle

An "engaging, funny and richly appreciative" (*The New York Times Book Review*) account of an English couple's first year living in Provence, settling in amid the enchanting gardens and equally festive bistros of their new home.

"Stylish, witty, delightfully readable."
—*The Sunday Times* (London)

Travel/0-679-73114-8/$10.00 (Can. $12.50)

Maiden Voyages: The Writings of Women Travelers
Edited and with an Introduction by Mary Morris

In this delightful and generous anthology, women such as Beryl Markham, Willa Cather, Annie Dillard, and Joan Didion share their experiences traveling throughout the world. From the Rocky Mountains to a Marrakech palace, in voices wry, lyrical, and sometimes wistful, these women show as much of themselves as they do of the strange and wonderful places they visit.

Travel/Women's Studies/0-679-74030-9/$14.00 (Can. $18.50)

Iron & Silk by Mark Salzman

The critically acclaimed and bestselling adventures of a young American martial arts master in China.

"Dazzling...exhilarating...a joy to read from beginning to end."
—*People*

Travel/Adventure/0-394-75511-1/$10.00 (Can. $13.50)

Available at your local bookstore or call toll-free to order: 1-800-733-3000 (credit cards only).
Prices subject to change.